MW01074069

What Did We Know?
What Did We Do?

Making Decisions in Large Organizations

By Fred Herzner

What Did We Know? What Did We Do? Making Decisions In Large Organizations

COPYRIGHT © 2017 Fred Herzner

Published by:
Smart Business Network
835 Sharon Drive, Suite 200
Westlake, OH 44145

Printed in the United States of America
Editor: Dustin S. Klein

ISBN: 978-1-945389-85-6

Library of Congress Control Number: 2017957173

Dedication

To the passengers and crew of United Airlines Flight 232, July 19, 1989.

Author's Note

In July 1989, United Airlines Flight 232 crashed in Sioux City, Iowa. In total, 111 people lost their lives and numerous others were seriously injured. The accident was initiated by a small metallurgical defect in an engine rotating part. That engine was manufactured by General Electric Aircraft Engines and I was the engineering manager of the group responsible for that part.

This is not a book about the accident. Rather, it is broader than that. This is a story about big, catastrophic events, the decisions that lead up to them, and their resulting consequences. It is also about the things that influence people and organizations to do what they do.

I bring a unique perspective to this because, for several years before the UA 232 accident, I was part of a team that was working on the problem that initiated the event. That deeply affected me. It drove me to look back at what I and others knew prior to the accident to try to understand why this terrible event happened.

Of course, after the accident, there was a flurry of activity to prevent further incidents and determine the root cause of the failure. But what I wanted to know was what underlying factors influenced the people and the organizations to fail to break the chain of events which led up to it. I was particularly focused on my own experience because I felt that had I done something differently, I might have changed the outcome.

Six years after the disaster, I was named the chief engineer of GE Aircraft Engines. Part of that responsibility was to manage the Flight Safety Organization, which had an advisory role on product safety matters. This gave me an opportunity to help structure a formal product safety policy based on my retrospective look at the Sioux City experience.

Then, after my retirement from GE in 2003, I started to see numerous devastating events in the news. These included the BP oil spill, the Flint, Michigan, lead-tainted water scandal, the General Motors ignition switch issue, and the Volkswagen diesel emissions cheating event.

From what I could see and read in the media, these events seemed to have been influenced by some of the same factors that led to the Sioux City accident. But some of these events had influencing factors which were not present in the UA 232 case. In fact, some of those factors were things I had never even thought about during my work tenure.

This made me think that perhaps I could help other organizations benefit not only from what I had learned from UA 232, but also from those recent events as well. So, I examined them and added some of the lessons learned to a set of principles which organizations could use to hopefully avoid such disasters.

Events like these have grave consequences and change the lives of many people. All the organizations that were involved—GE, BP, and VW, among others—paid dearly. Not only in financial terms, but also in loss of reputation. What I didn't expect was that the people inside those organizations who made the decisions also suffered consequences. I know I did because of my involvement with the UA 232 accident. Those consequences are still with me today.

This is what motivated me to begin writing. In this book, I have attempted to use what I learned from Sioux City and other recent events to propose a set of principles which others can use to avoid similar terrible outcomes. I also want this book to serve as a reminder and motivator for those who work in large organizations that what they do, and how they do it, is important to everyone: the people who use the products; the organizations that make the products and provide jobs; and last, but not least, the employees themselves.

Fred Herzner
Cincinnati
October 2017

Chapter 1
The Big Leagues

The plane that crash-landed in Sioux City, Iowa, on July 19, 1989, was a DC-10-10, powered by GE CF6-6 engines. While this accident cost 111 people their lives, it also changed the lives of the survivors and families of the victims as well. It was a true tragedy. But in events like this, there not only are significant consequences for the victims and their families, but also for the corporations and the employees that produce the products.

The initial consequences for organizations are obvious: ruined reputation, serious financial loss, legal and regulatory sanctions, among other repercussions. But what about employees? Those consequences are a bit more subtle. That is because in cases where lives are lost, such as UA 232, the employees involved may also have doubts about what their role was prior to the event.

How do I know?

Because at the time of the Sioux City accident, I was the engineering manager at GE Aircraft Engines who was responsible for the part that failed. And, prior to the accident, I was a member of an engineering team that was working on an issue which eventually was shown to have initiated that failure.

I must have watched videos of the crash a hundred times. It was so intense that the only words I could think of to describe it were "doomsday event." Even today, I still think of the victims and their families.

Immediately after the accident, there was intense media coverage as well as much speculation about the cause. Along with that came what seemed like an army of investigators asking many questions. The chaos subsided relatively quickly, and within several months the National Transportation Safety Board had a firm grasp on the technical reasons why the accident happened. All of this was followed by nine years of litigation, which served to keep those of us who were involved reminded of the tragedy.

I recognized that the technical questions had been answered, but I wanted to know what factors caused myself and the others involved to miss our chance to break the chain of events which led to the accident. GE, United Airlines, and McDonnell Douglas were some of the best companies in the world. I knew that at GE we always tried to do the right thing. Everyone knew safety was of the highest priority, and I never saw anything that would indicate a lack of responsibility or willingness to compromise that. Why did this happen then?

To find an answer, I decided to look back before the accident to see what we knew and what we did—or didn't do—about what we knew. Specifically, I wanted to understand the underlying reasons why the people and organizations made the decisions we did and to learn from this so we could avoid such tragic events in the future.

Once again, I learned the lesson that hindsight is wonderful. I found numerous factors that might have influenced us to not recognize the threats. That was true not only at GE, but by others in the industry. This encouraged me to dig deeper into exploring the "why" and "how" decisions get made.

For obvious reasons, I was particularly interested in the things I felt influenced me to do what I did. This is what the book you hold in your hands is all about: big organizations involved in big projects which, if they go wrong, could have catastrophic consequences for not only the victims, but the organizations and its employees. It is why I call them doomsday events. This book also explores how and why people in those organizations make decisions, and what needs to be done to help them make decisions which avoid such terrible consequences.

There are three reasons why I thought I could bring a unique perspective to this very complex subject.

First, I lived through one of these events. Prior to the accident, I was one of several people who may have had an opportunity to break the chain of events that led up to the UA 232 disaster. After the event, I was there to see and feel the consequences.

Second, I have immersed myself in aviation since I was a child. I built model airplanes, became an instrument and commercial rated pilot, built several experimental airplanes, and for 38 years worked as an aircraft engine engineer. Airplanes are my passion, and there is almost nothing about them I don't like. They have provided me with an understanding that, along with the joys of flight, comes a certain level of risk. That brings a responsibility to do everything reasonably possible to mitigate those risks. Every pilot knows this. If they are any good, they treat every airplane they fly and every flight they make with respect. Those who are not capable or willing to recognize these realities are destined to suffer serious consequences.

Third, I am not a psychologist. I'm an engineer. But I was an employee inside one of the biggest, best, and most complicated organizations in the world. As a result, I absorbed its culture; I watched its management; and I reveled in its technology. During my years at GE, I rose from being a working-level engineer to becoming chief engineer. I saw how big organizations work from the inside. I also learned that large organizations, like GE, are always on a big stage: They are working on complicated projects on the cutting edge of technology; their products have an impact on many people; huge sums of money are involved; and their actions are heavily scrutinized. I always thought we were in the "Yankee Stadium" of businesses. And because of that, I—and those around me—were in the big leagues.

However, when you're in the big leagues, you also have an opportunity to make big mistakes. Because of that, when I was chief engineer and responsible for the Flight Safety Organization, I took the opportunity to apply what I learned from the UA 232 experience to try to improve the process we used to address issues that might adversely impact product safety. That, too, was a learning experience as I discovered that theories are one thing but bringing them to practice is another.

Since I retired in 2003, I have thought about writing a book about all of this, but I always found a reason not to start. Then another very big event was reported in the media that I immediately classified as a doomsday event: the BP oil spill into the Gulf of Mexico.

As I read about it, I couldn't believe how serious the consequences were: 11 lives lost, a huge impact on the environment, and damages for BP in excess of $40 billion. As I reflected upon it, my thought was that if BP had implemented some of the lessons learned from the UA 232 event, perhaps the spill may not have occurred.

Following the BP oil spill, another big media story broke regarding fatalities—this time due to an ignition switch problem on certain model GM cars. The media portrayed it as a case where GM knew about the issue and chose not to take the appropriate action to protect its customers.

I was fascinated because it seemed to be a case where what appeared at first glance to be a minor issue turned out to be an event with significant consequences. Then came the Flint, Michigan, lead-tainted water and the VW diesel emissions scandal events. What "influence factors" were at work there? Were they the same or were there others I had not yet encountered?

Suddenly, I realized that not only did these events keep happening, but there were different reasons for why Flint and VW happened. By looking into them further, it broadened my horizons. I concluded these two were caused by behavior that was, in the case of VW, unethical, and in the case of Flint, immoral.

I was shocked! It was beyond comprehension that responsible people would do such things. That was all the motivation I needed to start writing. So, with that in mind, I used all five events—Sioux City, the BP oil spill, the GM ignition switch, Flint, Michigan's water crisis, and VW's diesel emissions cheating—as the basis to develop a set of principles intended for organizations to use to avoid the doomsday event.

Chapter 2
The Doomsday Event

When the United Airlines Flight 232 accident happened, it struck me like a bolt out of the blue. Almost immediately, the investigation team suspected that the fan disc in the front of the tail engine was the source of the problem that started the event. The fan disk was made from titanium—the material we had been working on for several years trying to solve a problem called "hard alpha". As time passed, I must have watched the video showing the left wing hitting the ground and the plane bursting into flames hundreds of times. Each time, I asked myself the same question: How could this have happened?

We were working on the hard alpha problem and we thought we were doing the right things. Yes, there were engine failures, but they never caused an accident. Never did I think I would have been involved with an event of this magnitude.

The news got even worse as details of the event began to surface: Children were killed. Wives lost husbands. Husbands lost wives. It was hard to comprehend—and even harder to accept.

As time passed, the true impact of the event became more apparent. In total, 111 people died. There were engines in the field that had to be managed. There were government agencies that had to be satisfied. There were customers who wanted to know what they needed to do. And all of this was taking place against a backdrop where the media questioned the safety of air travel, including flying United Airlines, traveling on McDonnell- Douglas airplanes, and aircraft that used GE Engines. As if that weren't enough to deal with, there soon began what would be nine years of litigation. This was my definition of a doomsday event: An unexpected catastrophic event caused by something that was known about and which led to serious consequences for the organizations and people involved.

In recent years, there were a series of events that exhibited the same characteristics: the BP oil spill into the Gulf of Mexico; the GM ignition switch problem; the VW diesel emissions "cheating" scandal; and the Flint, Michigan, lead-tainted water issue. In every case, these disasters were unexpected, involved large organizations, and had dire consequences for everybody. But, had warning signs prior to the event been listened to, the events may not have happened and the calamitous consequences could have been avoided.

In the case of the BP oil spill, BP and its contractors tried to drill oil wells deep in the ocean floor. They made poor decisions relative to how to cap the well. Eleven people were killed and a massive environmental disaster followed. It was unexpected at the BP corporate level, but those involved with the capping effort knew there was the potential for large-scale issues with their approach. As a result, BP was hit with huge costs for cleanup efforts, faced massive fines for its actions, and suffered an irreparable loss of reputation.

The GM ignition switch problem had some parallels with the UA 232 event in that GM knew of an ignition switch problem long before the first fatality occurred. They were working on a fix, but did not foresee that the problem would cause any fatalities. Then the first death occurred, and the company didn't react quickly enough to rectify the situation before things got out of control. The media sunk its teeth into the coverage, which led to Congressional hearings, unprecedented product recalls, and litigation. Once more, the loss of life—unexpected but with ample warnings that it was possible—resulted into a loss reputation and big financial and legal implications. It was terrible for the victims, bad for the corporation, and problematic for those individuals within the organization who were involved in the decision-making process.

The last two events—involving VW and Flint, Michigan—expanded my horizons as I thought about doomsday events. That was because both events involved what I judged to be unethical behavior. Never in my wildest dreams would I have expected a globally recognized organization to be involved in a cheating scandal. Why would government employees decide to risk the health of everybody in the city when they knew that the new source of water was 12 times more corrosive than before?

I believe that those at the top of both organizations were surprised that these catastrophic events occurred, though they are not without their own faults, but there certainly were folks inside these organizations who knew exactly what they were doing—and that it was wrong. That's what makes these two doomsday events very different from UA 232, GM, or BP. Despite that, they had similar results: huge loss of reputation, serious financial impact, and even the threat of incarceration for the employees involved.

In some respects, doomsday events caused by unethical behavior have even more disastrous effects than those caused by product safety issues. You might be forgiven for design errors, but you won't be forgiven if you cheat!

In every case, however, they are very serious events caused by mistakes made by large organizations. These events surprise almost everyone—including upper management—

but there is always someone inside the organization who knew about or was working on the problem which eventually caused it.

The other characteristic of doomsday events is that there are always very serious consequences for not only the victims, but for the organizations and the people in those organizations that were involved. As someone who was involved in such an event, I can attest that its effects will be felt by all for the remainder of their lives.

Chapter 3
United Airlines Flight 232

Wednesday, July 19, 1989, was a beautiful day across the country. In Denver, 296 passengers and crew members boarded a United Airlines DC-10-10 for a flight to Chicago. The flight was uneventful until a point just west of Sioux City, Iowa, when suddenly a large explosion occurred in the rear section of the airplane.

The DC-10-10 is a wide body aircraft manufactured by McDonnell Douglas and powered by General Electric engines. The airplane is a bit unusual in that two of the engines are mounted on the wing while the third is mounted in the tail section just above the horizontal surface of the tail (See Figure 1). When the explosion happened, everyone on board was alarmed. But what they and the crew didn't know was that a structural rotating part (called a fan disc) in the rear engine failed, rupturing three hydraulic lines which were routed through the horizontal stabilizer (See Figure 2).

One of the built-in failsafe mechanisms in the DC-10-10 is a triple redundant hydraulic control system designed so that failure of one, or even two, of the systems still allows the crew to control the airplane. Unfortunately, the debris from the fan disc hit all three hydraulic lines, effectively making the airplane uncontrollable.

After the failure, the crew watched as the hydraulic system pressures dropped to zero and the engine instrumentation indicated that the tail engine had failed. Suddenly, they realized that what they thought was a bad problem was really one that threatened the lives of everyone on board. What followed was one of the greatest feats of flying skill and cockpit resource management ever recorded.

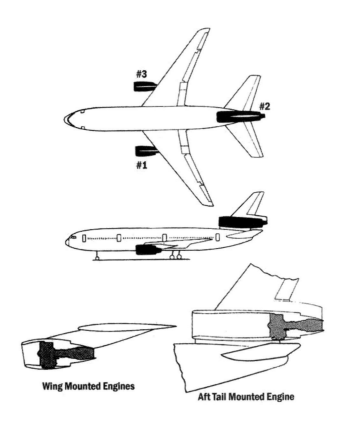

Figure 1. DC10 Tail Engine Position

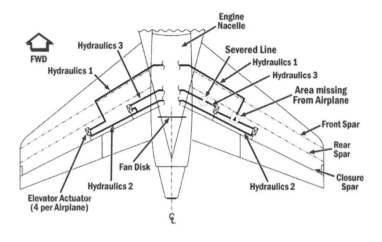

Figure 2a. Horizontal Stabilizer damage (diagram)

Figure 2b. Horizontal Stabilizer damage (photo)

13

As Captain Al Haynes struggled to learn how to fly an essentially uncontrollable airplane, Denny Fitch, a United Airlines DC-10 training check captain who was seated in the first-class cabin, recognized the seriousness of the situation and volunteered to come up to the cockpit to help. Captain Haynes immediately agreed.

After assessing the situation, the two men decided their best course of action was to use the only control device they had left—the two wing engines. Captain Haynes would manipulate the airplane's controls (which were not working) and plan for the landing while Check Captain Fitch moved the engine throttles in an attempt to control the airplane. This had never been done before and they recognized the chances of success were slim at best.

As time went on, the two men developed a plan for landing at Sioux City, Iowa. When asked later why he chose Sioux City as the place to land, Captain Haynes, recognizing he had no control over the airplane, replied, "That was the airport that the airplane wanted to go."

Despite their heroic efforts, the best Haynes and Fitch could do was make what could be described as a crash landing on a closed runway in Sioux City. Unfortunately, in doing so, 111 of the 296 people on board the flight lost their lives.

That afternoon, my boss and I were driving home from work at GE Aircraft Engines. As we listened to the news about the plane crash, we learned there was an engine failure which had damaged the airplane. We knew that United Airlines' DC-10-10's were powered by GE CF6-6 engines. Since both of us had been working on the CF6 engine family, we suspected there was a chance that one of the parts we were responsible for might be involved.

This was the first time it crossed my mind that I might have had something to do with this. Sure, there had been engine failures before, but nobody got hurt. This was totally different! Was I responsible in any way for this tragedy? Was there something I should have done differently to prevent it? Questions flooded my mind. Needless to say, there was not too much conversation in the car the rest of the way home.

The post-crash investigation quickly confirmed that the cause of the control system damage was the failure of the fan disc which holds the large rotating fan blades at the front of the engine *(See Figures 3, 4, and 5)*. The fan blades and disc were nowhere to be found near the crash site. They were apparently lost somewhere over the corn fields of Iowa. A search to find the disc fragments began so that they could be examined and confirm—or dispel—the initial suspicions.

Figure 3. Fan Disc photo

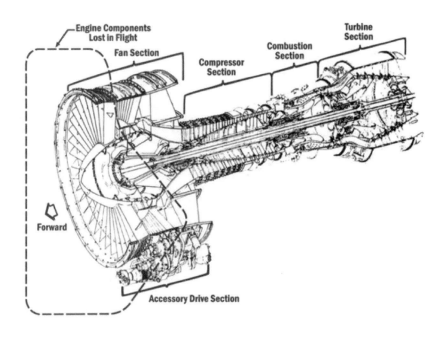

Figure 4. Engine Cross Section

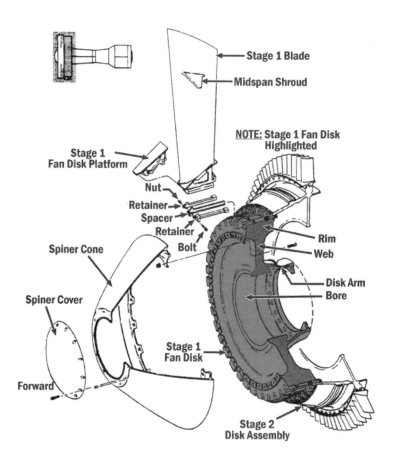

Figure 5. Rotor assembly drawing

As part of the investigation back at GE, we recovered the manufacturing and use records for the fan disc that was in the tail engine.

According to the service records, the disc was manufactured in 1971 and, in more than 18 years of service, had flown for 41,009 hours and 15,503 flights. We also learned that the disc had been inspected numerous times in the airline overhaul shop. The last time was 760 flights (about one year) before the accident. At that time, it was determined to be OK to return to service.

Since the failed disc itself was not yet found, we went to the airlines to recover five other fan discs that were made from the same titanium billet as the failed part. They were significant because, having come from the same billet, they were made from the same metal as the failed disc. None of these discs were found cracked, but a cut-up examination of one of them was performed at GE's metallurgical laboratory in Evendale, Ohio.

In August, one month after the crash, I was walking across the parking lot at the plant on a hot afternoon when I ran into the metallurgist I had been working with on the investigation. He was holding a cut-up cross section of one of these sister discs. It showed very conclusively the billet that this disc and the failed disc had been made from had a very unusual microstructure. That was an indication there was a serious problem with the melting process used to make the metal. Both of us immediately knew there was a high probability that the titanium issue we had been working on might be related to the failure. It is hard to convey the feeling that I got in the pit of my stomach. Welcome to the big leagues!

Eventually, pieces of the failed disc were found confirming that the cause was a metallurgical defect. The chain of events that led up to the accident started to take shape. It began with a defect in the titanium, followed by inspections both at manufacture and in the airline shop that did not find the defect. This, coupled with the airplane design that placed all three hydraulic lines in a vulnerable position formed the "chain of events" that eventually led to the crash.

Had any one of these links been broken, the accident would not have happened.

In the aftermath of the event, it became apparent we needed to develop an immediate plan to mitigate the existing risk on other airplanes and engines that were in service. This was our short-term containment plan. Then, once we were sure there was something in place to keep other engines safe, we needed to address the process issues that were the true underlying cause of the failure. This was a much more difficult task and took substantially longer to accomplish because it meant improving the processes used to melt and inspect titanium.

There were other long-term process improvements that would be needed to close the gap. They would have to address:

- The placement of control systems in airplanes to keep them from being damaged by debris should an engine fail.
- Improving the inspection techniques so that metallurgical defects could be found prior to getting into finished parts.
- Finding new ways to inspect critical parts in the overhaul shops so that they were not subject to "human factors."

Obviously, there were significant financial and legal consequences that followed the event. UA 232 carried with it substantial liabilities for all the companies involved. I experienced some of that as well when I participated in a deposition in a Chicago courtroom where both my personal integrity and the integrity of the company I worked for were called into question. Neither my education as an engineer nor considering myself a responsible person prepared me well for that moment.

If you stand back and look at the Sioux City accident, the chain of events that led up to it was incredibly long and complicated. Building large commercial airplanes and engines requires many sophisticated processes and unique technologies.

In addition, it requires a complicated network of companies and their employees, who are focused on the specific part of the process for which they are responsible. If there is a problem in one area, it is up to the overall system to mitigate the risk.

However, that system depends on the state-of-the-art technology available at the time when the airplanes and engines were manufactured and built. The flight UA 232 airplane and engines were designed in the 1960s, built in the '70s, and inspected in the '80s. The safety record for commercial aviation in those years was significantly worse than it is today. Those safety improvements were made possible by applying what was learned from the earlier experience. And that is what this book is all about.

Later on, we will look at one part of the chain of events that led up to the UA 232 event to try to identify the gaps that allowed the metallurgical defect to slip through the system. I'll also provide a view as to what my role was while working on the titanium defect problem and how sometimes subtle influences can lead to decisions which prevent the links in the chain from being broken. This experience is what I started me on my journey to see what could be done to improve the way we addressed potential product safety issues at GE Aircraft Engines. It is also the reason I became interested in the "why" and the "how" I, and others in large, complex organizations, make decisions which may have unexpected and significant consequences.

Chapter 4
Then and Now

I graduated from high school in 1959. My family lived in a section of New York City that was centrally located between LaGuardia and Idlewild airports (now JFK), and Floyd Bennett Field (New York's first commercial airport, and later a Naval base in Brooklyn). I watched airplanes all the time. I also read the newspapers and took note of all the accidents. Unfortunately, there was never a lot of wait time in between air disasters.

One particular accident stands out: a collision over Brooklyn of a four-engine commercial jet DC-8 with a four-engine reciprocating Lockheed L-10490 Super Constellation—one of the most beautiful airplanes of all time—as they were attempting to land at LaGuardia. The DC-8 came to rest in the Park Slope section of Brooklyn and the Constellation fell on Staten Island. As a result, 134 people were killed.

I saw pictures of the wreck in the newspaper, but after a day or two, it seemed to disappear. In those days, airplane accidents were accepted as a reality and not completely unexpected. People accepted that there was a finite risk when you stepped onto an airplane. Some were willing to take that risk; others were not.

When I began my career at GE in 1965, I met a very smart engineer who worked in the same department. One day, she and her husband flew to the United Kingdom for a vacation. They never returned. When we found out about the airplane accident, it seemed like everyone in the office just shrugged their shoulders and accepted that this was the way things were. That is not the case today.

A report by Boeing chronicling commercial jet airplane accidents from 1959 through 2015 revealed that the fatal accident rate in 1959 was 40 per million departures. Today, that number is virtually zero. People have become accustomed to a new normal and are unwilling to accept the kinds of risks that were generally accepted in the past.

On the ethical side, it is the same. In the past, breaches of ethical conduct by a bank or a business were generally considered local events. Only a limited number of people were impacted or even aware of them. Today's highly connected world has created a completely different environment. The Wells Fargo unauthorized account doomsday event is a perfect example.

The point here is events that were once accepted because they had limited impact no longer go unnoticed or accepted. Today's events are fully capable of having dire consequences for the organizations and in some cases the individuals that are involved. This is also reflected in the liability judgments associated with every disaster. The financial impact of the BP oil spill, for example, was in excess of $40 billion; the VW emissions cheating scandal will cost the company in excess of $20 billion.

There is another a very significant difference between the past and the present—we live in a digital world. As I was researching the Flint, Michigan, lead-tainted water event, I was struck by how much detail the internet provided. It was like watching a bad movie. The legal disclosure process after the Sioux City accident involved more than 300,000 pages of documentation—all of which had to be read to separate the relevant documents from the non-relevant ones. Obviously,

that was a very difficult task and did not provide an,
near the clarity the Flint emails did.

While the world has changed, what hasn't chang
the basic requirements necessary for how an organizatic
must do business—professionally and responsibly in all
forms of communication and documentation. It should be
a given that any and all documentation and communication
will be uncovered should a doomsday event occur. There is
no place left to hide anything that may indicate whether the
organization or its employees were acting irresponsibly or
with malicious intent. If you still don't believe me, when you
read about the Flint, Michigan, lead in the water event in
Chapter 12, look at the timeline that details how it unfolded.

In the old days, I would carry with me a bound daily
log which I used as a reminder of meeting conclusions and
a mobile "to-do list." I carried it around for years, including
the period leading up to the UA 232 event. I was relatively
casual about how I recorded things. Not that they were
bad, but they were not intended to be seen by anyone but
myself. After the accident, we had to produce every scrap
of documentation that we had relative to the accident. So, I
went through my log and made copies of anything that had
to do with the hard alpha/titanium problem that I had been
working on.

I was particularly sensitive to one page that contained
a very terse note that I wrote when I came out of the
review with the chief engineer about hard alpha. It simply
said something like "inspect fan discs." The rest of the log
included items such as personnel management issues and
other things which had nothing to do with the event.

Prior to a deposition in Chicago, I provided copies of
any of the pages relevant to the hard alpha issue to the legal

.m. Then, during the deposition in Chicago, I was asked to produce the entire log. I said "no" because it contained non-related information that I considered "mine." Needless to say, the log got turned over to the plaintiffs' attorneys. I guarantee that if you find yourself in a similar situation, you will want to be sure that what you recorded reflects well on both yourself and your organization.

Looking back—and taking everything that's occurred since then into account—I now recognize that achieving the goal of communicating and documenting professionally and respectfully is difficult. Sometimes, people do the strangest things. In the '60s I saw things in books used to record design calculations which were nothing short of shocking. A few even included foul language and cartoons. This shows that the people who did that never thought the material would be discovered or seen by anyone else. It is vital that all employees understand that they and their organization will be judged on how they communicate and document. This goal should, therefore, be one of the values communicated to all in the organization. And as such, it should become something that becomes ingrained in the organization's culture. It is important that management plays an active role in assuring that everyone in the organization understands that words and documents matter—they really matter.

Chapter 5
Money and Values -
The Elephants in the Room

There are few things that influence the way we make decisions more than money. Money is the way things get done. It is the fuel on which the economy runs. Because of that, money empowers people and organizations to do what they need—and want—to do. This can be both good and bad. As individuals, having money puts food on the table, provides shelter, and educates our children. It provides everything we need to lead a good quality of life. For corporations, money is the reason they are in business. They have salaries to pay, factories to build, products to design and sell, and investors to satisfy. For governments, tax money allows them to build the infrastructure needed to provide for the common good. All of this is beneficial.

Because money is such an important influence on everyone's lives, it can also be a very powerful influence on how we choose to acquire and use it. Earning money by working hard and contributing to society are obviously good things. If someone chooses to be a thief or evade paying taxes, that's a bad thing. In each case, people make conscious decisions based on how they choose to live their lives and the environment that surrounds them (more on that later). Organizations, also, make similar choices when it comes to earning and spending money. This comes into play when they ponder how to price products, satisfy Wall Street's demands, and run their day-to-day operations.

Since money is quantifiable, it is how things get done and are measured. You either have enough to buy the car or you don't. You either met the measurement or you didn't—no interpretation is necessary. I like to think of money as an enabler (it allows you to do what you want to do) and a means of measuring success or failure. All of this makes the "money elephant" very powerful. There is no question that it will be heard when organizations or the people in them make decisions. It is sheer fantasy to think otherwise.

Certainly, money has earned its reputation as being "the root of all evil" and having enticed many people to do some terrible things in their quest to get it. Since money is an enabler, if you have it, you also have a powerful resource to do good. I learned this when I was an engineer at GE Aircraft Engines and faced a potential safety issue. It was very nice to work for a company that had the resources and the will to spend them to solve problems. Money is not the root of all evil. It is organizations, people, and the way they choose to acquire and spend money that determines whether money is evil or a means to do good.

When it comes to doomsday events, there are two other elephants in the room besides money. Doomsday events are almost always associated with failure to either supply safe products or do business in an ethical manner. Nobody will get into a car or an airplane that is proven to have safety issues. Few will do business with a company that lies about its products or cheats. This makes ethical behavior and product safety "elephants." But are they as influential as the money elephant, or are they silent? The reality is managers don't come in every morning and tell the employees to build safe products or not. These things are generally not discussed. Everyone is expected to "just know" this is the way they are expected to do business. This is why both are silent elephants.

If doomsday events are to be avoided, it is vital that the value elephants (product safety and ethical behavior) be heard at least as much as the money elephant when making decisions which potentially threaten the existence of the organization. In a word, they must be "balanced."

But what does balanced mean?

In the case of ethical behavior, the answer is relatively simple: a strict adherence to laws and regulations and doing business in a manner that values the welfare of the customer above that of the organization. In a few words: legal and fair.

In the case of product safety, the answer is not as easy because there are two factors that complicate the relationship between money and product safety: risk and how to place a value on human life.

How many times have you heard or read that you cannot put a value on human life? Taking this literally, it would mean that there could be no discussion of money when deciding how to mitigate even the smallest threats. Personally, I know of no case where difficult projects get done or high-tech products get developed without involving either risk or money. Every time you get in an airplane, you take a risk. You can't drill oil wells thousands of feet below the ocean floor with no risk. Building airplanes and drilling for oil takes a lot of money. This makes the money elephant and product safety elephant unavoidably intertwined. Unfortunately, that makes balancing decisions exceptionally difficult.

What then does "balanced" mean when product safety is involved? The only answer that I have—and it is admittedly not a good one—is that a decision is balanced when, after an event, it is judged by others to be reasonable, responsible, and reflect appropriate concern for the health and welfare of the users. It's a definition that unfortunately is very subjective and the meaning of the words "reasonable," "responsible," and "appropriate concern" can be left open to a wide range of interpretations.

Despite its vagaries, I believe this definition gives good guidance as to how product safety decisions should get made. My thought is that "reasonable" means the decisions make sense; "responsible" means it was made using a disciplined process, weighed against defined criteria, and reviewed by independent and knowledgeable people; and "appropriate concern" means the organization made significant effort to mitigate the risk at considerable cost to itself.

Remember, however, should a doomsday event occur, the judgments of reasonable, responsible, and the like are made by people outside the organization—victims, victims' families, lawyers, governments, and regulators. After an event, the organization and the people in it do not get a vote. They already had their opportunity to judge "balanced" when they were deciding what to do—and what not to do. This is precisely the reason why they must not let the pressing, day-to-day focus on financial issues outweigh their responsibility to adhere to and protect the underlying values of the enterprise. If they fail to do so, the consequences will be harsh—not only for the organization, but for the people themselves.

With all of this in mind, let's turn now to look at one of the most influential factors that influences people and organizations to make decisions: organizational culture.

Chapter 6
Organizational Culture

The term organizational culture is a lot harder to define than the elephants in the room. Like those elephants—often overlooked, but present and seldom heard from—culture is rarely discussed because there is nothing tangible to talk about. Organizational culture is a feeling which is developed throughout time while working with or inside an organization. At its most basic level, culture is the way individuals judge what their surrounding world considers acceptable behavior. More simply put, it is the way things get done inside an organization.

All of us live in a number of surrounding worlds: the nation, our family, our circle of friends, and the company we work for. Together, these comprise our daily environment and, although each embodies different goals and standards, they all influence how we judge acceptable behavior.

The national goal is to defend the country and provide for the common good. Acceptable behavior is to obey the law and conduct business in an ethical manner.

Families have goals more limited in scope but generally are to provide a home, food, and a nurturing environment for children. Acceptable behavior in the family world may or may not be what the outside world considers acceptable. The father or mother may set a poor example for the children; it really depends on the culture within each respective family unit.

Our circle of friends may have an even wider range of goals and standards that they use to define acceptable behavior. Some of those might be good—like a strong work ethic or high moral standards—and others might not be so good—like making poor decisions or cheating at sports. As with anything else, acceptability is in the eye of the beholder.

Finally, in a lot of ways, companies are similar to families—they establish goals and standards for what is considered acceptable behavior. However, unlike the family unit, a large organization may have sub-families with sub-goals and sub-standards. One sub-family—a department, for example—might be measured on product function while another sub-family is measured on product cost. This leads to a different perception of what is acceptable behavior. Consider it from this perspective: A person in the manufacturing organization might see others around him getting rewarded for compromising quality to improve yield. Seeing that, he might be led to believe this behavior is the norm in that environment. Accordingly, it defines the culture of that specific sub-family.

Messages sent by the organization's leadership are also very powerful influences on culture. If the CEO's words or actions communicate that goals are to be achieved at "all costs" without communicating that no compromise will be made relative to the ethics and product safety "elephants," the entire family will get the message. That will lead to a single-mindedness when it comes to decision-making, bringing those inside the organization to the mindset where they feel it is OK to take risks to meet their established goals.

In 1965, I joined GE's Evendale, Ohio-based jet propulsion division as a young design engineer. I knew that GE was one of the largest and most influential companies in the world, but I had no idea how it functioned or how it was managed. GE's jet propulsion division was in the business of making jet engines, mostly for military applications, but working hard to develop products for commercial use. (At this point in time, it's important to note that the commercial jet airliner was relatively new—having begun regular service around 1959.) The company—like many of its competitors—was pursuing new concepts, and the technology both on the engine and airframe side was rapidly advancing. This was exciting work for a young engineer, especially since it involved airplanes and engines.

I was surrounded with bright and talented engineers who had a "get-the-job-done" attitude. Looking around me, I also had the impression that these people were good people. Never during those early years did I ever pick up on any signs that doing business unethically would be tolerated or accepted. I did observe, however, that sometimes, formal processes or procedures would be "modified" in the interest of getting the job done. That, too, was part of the culture.

What feeling did I get from all of this?

To be frank, I liked it. It was exciting. What wasn't there to be excited about? I got to work on new products, try new things, and learn a lot in the process. What was it that I judged as acceptable behavior during that time at GE? It was pretty straightforward: support the product, work hard, and get things done. Did this feeling impact the way I made decisions or how I approached doing my job? You bet it did.

But what influenced how I judged the culture during those years? I listened to what the upper management said but, more importantly, I watched what they did. I looked at my peers and saw how they worked and how they were rewarded for what they did. Good engineers who got their jobs done well were rewarded. I liked what I saw and what I felt. It seemed to me that the organization's way of doing business was the way I thought it should be done.

So why is this important? It matters because it affected the way I did my job. I modeled my behavior after the behavior of those around me. And, when I was faced with making decisions, I tried to make those decisions the way I thought the organization wanted me to make them. The bottom line is that the organization's culture has a direct impact on what and how people do their jobs.

When we talked about values in the last chapter, the point was made that, to avoid doomsday events, the decisions that were made had to reflect the underlying core values of the organization—the balanced decision. It follows that, if the organization's culture affects how people do their jobs, then the culture must reflect those values also. The right culture is one that motivates employees to put the overarching interests of the users and organization above their own and reflects the values of ethical behavior and product safety. That is only possible if the words and actions of the entire management team send that message. In my view, culture is the way that the word "values" is translated into actions. Culture matters. It really matters.

Chapter 7
How and Why Decisions Are Made

Six things influence the way people and organizations make decisions: values, goals, culture, organizational complexity, measurements, and the perception of risk. Unfortunately, these factors are interrelated and depend upon the unique—and often diverse—individuals who are involved.

If a governor is elected on a platform of saving money, do you think that goal will influence the way decisions will be made in his administration? How about the case where a project is months late and grossly over budget? Will those measurements influence the decisions about how to complete the job? In a situation where upper management never talked about values but made it clear that goals have to be met, would employees do something illegal to meet those goals? You get the idea.

Any of these factors, if not all, can and do have a significant impact on how people make decisions.

We've discussed values and culture, so let's look at the others to see how they influence the decision-making process.

There are two forms of organizational complexity: inter-organization and intra-organization. In the case where multiple organizations are working together, each organization brings its own values, goals, cultures, and measurements. These factors interact in very complex ways. Add communication issues and contractual relationships into the mix, and it becomes clear that organizational complexity has a powerful influence on how decisions get made. (Look for this when we later examine the BP oil spill and the Flint, Michigan, lead-tainted water problem).

Even when there is only one organization, complexity can be a significant influence. This is because large organizations are made up of numerous sub-organizations, such as divisions, departments, and sections which have different goals, cultures, and measurements. Therefore, even though all those sub-organizations are under the same organizational umbrella, the "logo" is faced with complexity and communication issues as well.

Complexity also blurs the lines of responsibility. In retrospect, I believe it played a role in the UA 232 event. See if you agree when we go through the chain of events leading up to the accident and I describe the meeting between myself and the chief engineer. The lack of execution or follow-through is an important, yet difficult to manage, influence factor. If you think others are responsible, you may think you are not responsible. But if everybody is responsible, who has the final responsibility to act? Organizational complexity clearly makes answering this question difficult.

Let's look at goals. Unlike values, organizational goals are typically well communicated by upper management. Everyone knows what the organization wants to accomplish. Going back to my experience prior to the UA 232 event, I knew at GE Engines an important organizational goal was to achieve market share by providing airlines with the best customer support. This, in turn, shaped a culture which influenced the decisions I made when I did my job. This is a good example of how the goals and culture can influence decisions. It also illustrates how the six factors interact.

Measurements are another critical factor because they are the way employees and companies are judged. Measurements are what define success or failure and are far easier to focus in on than the two values—ethics and safety. This is because you can put a number on them. How many parts did we ship? How much cost did we remove from the process? How many did we sell? Did we meet the quarter? Needless to say, measurements have a very strong influence when one is trying to weigh one factor against another.

The final piece of the equation is perception of risk. There are two types. The first is where there is simply no recognition that something terrible could actually happen. This is the so called "black swan" event. The most common manifestation of this is where the thought process is "if it never happened before it can't happen." The second type is that there is the possibility of such an event, but a judgment is made about its chances of happening. That judgment is then weighed against the other factors to determine the course of action.

Having the right perception of risk is the Holy Grail of decision making. But, just like finding the Holy Grail, getting that right is extremely difficult. It is essentially predicting the future. With that said, decisions do have to be based on the best information available, and that information must include a judgment of the level of risk.

Of all the six factors, determining the level of risk is the most difficult and the most important. It is the most important because it determines whether action will be taken or an issue will be left up to the normal course of business. Whenever I found myself in this situation, I always hoped God would come down and tell me what to do. He never did!

In the following chapters, we will examine the events

which led up to several well-publicized doomsday events. The purpose is to look at what led up to those events and illustrate how the six factors influenced the outcomes. I will warn you, two of these events will probably make you shake your head and question what could possibly have brought some of these people to do what they did.

Chapter 8
UA232 - The Chain of Events

The chain of events that led up to the Sioux City accident did not start with the engine fan disc failure. Rather, it began long before that—during the melting process which created the titanium used to make the disc. While the process used to melt titanium is specialized, there are many similar processes used to manufacture complex, high-tech parts, which include steps which, if not done precisely right, have the potential to result in defects.

This may sound onerous, but it's not. It's fairly typical of any process which had not yet enjoyed the benefits of long periods of improvement and upgrade. Back in the early 1970s, when the UA 232 engine disc was made, the Kroll process used for manufacturing titanium was about 30 years old and still being improved.

Taking a further step back, there are no manufacturing processes which are free from potential problems—no matter how many safeguards are put into place. Even established manufacturing processes sometimes have known vulnerabilities but the people who use them have judged them to be the "best available" or "state of the art." In those cases, the vulnerabilities are addressed by careful attention to process control or by additional inspections. These types of scenarios more often come into play when the process depends on humans to do things that are either difficult or repetitive.

There were four significant links in the chain of events that led to the UA 232 disaster: the creation of the metallurgical defect in the disc that caused the failure; the failure of the inspection process used to look for defects at manufacture; the failure to find the crack when the disc was inspected at the engine overhaul shop; and the decision to locate all three hydraulic lines close together in the tail.

To understand how the UA 232 accident chain developed and how the links interacted, let's look at the titanium melting and inspection processes that were used during manufacture of the fan disc. Then we will look at how the parts were inspected when they were in the engine overhaul shop. This will give a better perspective on what was known about the type of defect that caused the disc to fail and what was being done to mitigate the risks associated with them. What did we know? What did we do?

It is important here to recognize that the "we" I am referring to is the "big we." It is anyone who had anything to do with the creation of the metal, the manufacture of the disc, and the maintenance/inspection at the overhaul shop. It is the people who were involved with melting the titanium. It is the people who machined the disc. It is the people in the overhaul shop who inspected it. It is the people who were involved with supporting the products that were in service. I was one of those people.

Everyone's job in the aviation industry is to recognize potential problems and do whatever is needed to achieve an acceptable level of safety. It is also important to recognize that, in most cases, people are focused on their own specific area of expertise and do not have a good perspective on how the vulnerabilities in their part of the process can potentially threaten the entire system. One might say "they miss the forest for the trees."

One more note: As you read through this, you might think that I am trying to make you an expert in how titanium is melted and inspected. This is not the case as the description here is quite simplified. Rather, the purpose is simply to illustrate how the chain developed and try to identify some of the important factors that were involved in influencing how decisions were made.

The process used to make titanium begins with an ore called rutile, which is reacted with chlorine to produce a clear liquid called "tickle" ($TiCl4$). "Tickle" is then reacted with sodium in a huge, hot caldron to form two solids—pure titanium and salt. Thinking back to high school chemistry, this reaction can be described by the equation $TiCl4 + 4Na = Ti + 4NaCl$.

Figure 6. Sponge

At the end of this process, the caldron is allowed to cool and the contents then solidify into a mixture of titanium (Ti) and salt (NaCl). The caldron is opened and the mixture is jackhammered out in big and small pieces that look a lot like rocks. The larger rocks are crushed down further and the salt is leached out of the mixture leaving pure titanium. At that point, the titanium looks exactly like sponge (as in a car washing sponge—*See Figure 6*). The titanium sponge is mixed with other alloying elements to give the appropriate chemistry for the alloy and then compacted into what are called bricks. The bricks, which are roughly the size of a typical cinder block, are then assembled into what is called a stick. A stick is large assembly of titanium sponge bricks which are then put into the melting furnace. Typically, the sticks look like a very large square pole, about 2 to 3 feet wide by 10 to 16 feet long.

The stick assembly is formed by stacking and welding the bricks together. At the time the UA 232 disc was manufactured, those welds were done under a small tent set up locally around the individual welds, and argon gas was put in to surround the weld as it was being made. Since argon is inert, this arrangement was intended to shield the hot molten weld from the oxygen in the air—a very important part of the process. Then, after all the welds are made, the stick assembly is placed into a vacuum furnace and melted (when the UA 232 disc was made, this was done twice) into an ingot. An ingot is about 2 to 3 feet in diameter and up to 10 feet long. Note that I said the tent filled with argon gas used in the welding of the stick assembly was very important. That is because titanium can be described as a "getter." A "getter" is a material that attracts oxygen when it is hot—as in a weld. So, the purpose of the tent filled with argon was to shield the hot titanium in the weld bead from the oxygen in the air.

However, if the tent does not keep all the air out, then the titanium "gets" the oxygen in the air and reacts with it to form what is called hard alpha. Unfortunately, hard alpha has the characteristic of being hard, brittle, weak, and sometimes voided. None of those characteristics are acceptable if contained in highly stressed parts, like engine fan discs.

There were also several other places in the melting process that had the potential for creating hard alpha. But, the post-accident investigation concluded that the most likely source of the problem was that the tent, which was supposed to be filled with argon, allowed air to leak in and react with the hot titanium in one of the welds.

The next step in the manufacture of the UA 232 fan disc was to extrude the ingot down to a billet. That process is akin to squeezing a tube of toothpaste. The titanium ingot was drawn down in diameter from 28 inches to 16 inches, making it look like a rod, which was about 20 feet long (*See Figure 7*). This step is important for a number of metallurgical reasons but, relative to hard alpha, the smaller the billet diameter, the greater the distortion and the greater the chances for cracking any hard alpha defects. This is important because hard alpha defects cannot be detected by the inspection processes used unless cracked or voided. It is for this reason that at this point in the process billets were subjected to what was called "contact ultrasonic inspection."

Figure 7. Billet

It is called "contact" because the sensing probe is passed directly over the billet's surface, and "ultrasonic" because the probe emits sound waves through the metal and senses the shape of the waves that are reflected back. If there is a crack or void that is large enough to distort the reflected waves, the defect can be detected.

The billet used to make the UA 232 disc passed the contact ultrasonic inspection.

The next step in the process is to cut the billet into "mults" (a mult is a piece of the billet large enough to make a disc), forge them and then machine them into a "rectilinear" shape that facilitates the next ultrasonic inspection. That inspection is made while immersed in water and is called "immersion ultrasonic." Doing it in fluids enhances the sensitivity of the inspection.

The UA 232 disc passed. It is unclear if it passed both ultrasonic inspections because the defect was not cracked or voided, or if the inspection processes used were simply not sensitive enough.

Following that, the discs were machined into the final part shape and inspected again using a process called "fluorescent penetrant inspection" or FPI. A rough description of the FPI process is that the part is cleaned and then dipped into a fluid which glows brightly when exposed to ultraviolet light. After it is dipped, fluid is gently removed from the surface and the part is visually inspected using ultraviolet light. If there are any cracks or voids on the surface, they will hold the fluid and glow under the light.

The UA 232 disc passed the FPI inspection as well and was sent out to be installed in an engine.

Here again, there are several important details to be noted. First and foremost, the FPI process could only detect defects that were on the surface. Second, the hard alpha had to be cracked or voided to hold the fluid and be detectable. Third, the FPI process depended on humans to both properly process the part and visually see any defects that were there.

In summary, the titanium material from which the UA 232 disc was made underwent a process which occasionally produced hard alpha defects. Finding those defects depended on the contact ultrasonic inspection of the billet, the immersion ultrasonic inspection of the "rectilinear" shape of the disc, and the FPI inspection of the final part shape. All of these inspections required the hard alpha defect to be cracked or voided to be detectable. This was typical of the way titanium parts were made in the 1970s—the so-called "industry standard."

In the early '70s, there were two versions of the CF6 high bypass turbofan engine. One was the CF6-6, which powered the DC-10-10; and the CF6-50, which powered the DC-10-30 and the Boeing 747. The two designs were very similar and both used titanium in the fan discs and forward part of the high-pressure compressor. Because they powered several airplane models, they began accumulating a lot of service hours.

Then, in 1974, the first of a number of titanium rotating part failures due to hard alpha occurred. It was an in-flight failure of a CF6-50 high pressure compressor spool. The titanium used in those spools was produced by the same process described above. The failure was considered serious because metal fragments exited the engine cases. Fortunately, the airplane landed safely and nobody was hurt. Following that event, there were several improvements made to the melting and inspection processes, but the basic processes themselves remained the same.

Five years later, in 1979, there was another failure of a CF6-50 high pressure compressor spool with essentially the same result. Again, the airplane landed safely. Additional improvements were made to the melting and inspection processes. This included adding an immersion ultrasonic inspection of the high-pressure compressor spool to the FPI inspection that was previously used when engine came into the shop for overhaul.

To understand why this was done and why it was significant, look at the design of the high-pressure compressor spool (*See Figure 8*). Since the FPI inspection is visual, the person doing the inspection must look inside the barrel-like spool to be able to detect any indications. This was accomplished with a mirror, which made it more difficult. The immersion ultrasonic inspection used a probe that was run over the surface of the part and the readout was done electronically. It does not depend on a human to "see" the defect.

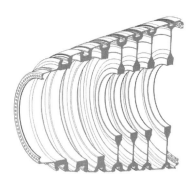

Figure 8. CF6-50 Compressor Spool

At that time, an immersion ultrasonic inspection was not put in place for fan discs. This was done for two reasons: first, there had never been any problem with fan discs; and second, the geometry of the fan disc allowed an inspector (using the FPI process) to see the entire surface of the part without using a mirror. This left the FPI inspection—the one which would be done at the United Airlines overhaul shop—as the final opportunity to break the last link in the chain of events which led up to the UA 232 accident.

Around the same time, back at GE, engineers began trying to quantify the level of risk posed by the hard alpha problem. Basically, it was an attempt to try to put numbers on the chances a hard alpha defect would be created and go undetected by the processes that were in place. This is not unusual in the aviation industry as assessments like this can dictate the scope and timing of the action plan to work out a potential safety issue. In this case, the problem was akin to finding a needle in a haystack: The needle refers to an undetected hard alpha defect large enough to cause a failure, while the haystack is the amount of titanium which made up the parts. An additional challenge was there were multiple haystacks, depending on the specific vendor that melted the titanium, the time period during which the material was made, and the inspection processes used.

The field experience on the CF6-50 compressor spools told us there was a possibility of such a defect getting into the parts, but we did not know how many defects there were, how big they were, and most importantly, where they were. Needless to say, it was a very difficult and frustrating task.

The burden of addressing this dilemma fell to a few experts in the materials engineering and quality control areas, along with the people at the titanium suppliers. They collected the available data and began assessing the risk levels in an attempt to improve the accuracy of the calculations.

This entire effort proved problematic because of the limited capability of the inspection processes used at the time the parts were manufactured and the process variations encountered at the different titanium melting sources. We eventually concluded the results were not valid and decided to concentrate our efforts on improving the melting and inspection processes.

In June 1983, there was a third CF6-50 spool failure, followed a week later by the failure of another titanium part—the Stage 1 disc area of a Stage 1-2 spool of a CFM-56 engine on a DC-8-71 aircraft (*See Figure 9*). Again, there were no injuries. However, the events were serious enough to expel metal debris from the engine. Two failures this close together attracted a lot of attention.

There were three reasons why the CFM-56 failure was different than earlier failures. First, and most worrisome, was that the originating defect was significantly larger than anyone ever expected. None of the previous data analysis or inspection results indicated that a defect of this size could have ever escaped—but it did. Second, the defect was completely below the surface of the part, making it undetectable by any visual process (like FPI). Third, the ultrasonic inspection done in the factory failed to detect the defect, meaning it was likely not cracked or voided when it was inspected.

This led to the conclusion that the only way to reliably find hard alpha defects was to inspect them after they had been exposed to in-service stresses which would crack/void the defect. In other words, inspect them at the airlines' shops. We were confident that if the field plan were aggressive enough, the inspection programs we were putting in place would be effective in preventing more failures. The challenge would be finding any cracked parts in the overhaul shop before they could lead to a failure.

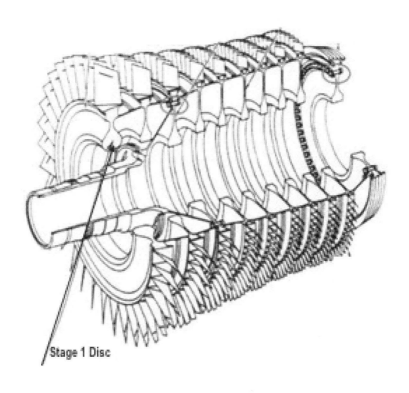

Figure 9. CFM 56 Compressor Rotor

Along with enhancing our field inspection plan, we recognized the basic issues with the melting and inspection processes needed to be addressed. A special team was formed, and I was assigned to it as part of my responsibilities as manager of fan and compressor engineering. This was the first time I was exposed to the details of making titanium.

Our team's primary focus was to develop and implement a melting process which did not produce hard alpha defects. This effort eventually resulted in what is now called hearth melting. Unfortunately, the process required the melters to buy new furnaces, which significantly delayed its introduction. It was nearly a full decade before significant quantities of hearth-melted titanium were incorporated into engine parts.

Concurrently, the inspection processes were addressed. Ultrasonic inspection capabilities were greatly improved and defects significantly smaller than those which could be found in the 1970s would eventually become detectable both in the field and during production. Improvements to the FPI process were not made until digital imaging techniques were available, making it less prone to human error. Most of these improvements were not available between 1983 and 1989.

Sometime in 1985, I had the opportunity to brief the then chief engineer on what we were doing about the hard alpha problem. We reviewed the field experience and our approach to minimizing the risk of additional failures. During that briefing, he asked how compressor spools and fan discs were being inspected.

I explained the spools were being inspected using immersion ultrasonic and FPI techniques, but the fan discs were only being FPI inspected. He suggested we add the immersion ultrasonic inspection to the fan disc program. I made an appropriate note in my "To Do" log, and went back to my office.

Following the meeting, I called the manager of the product support organization and relayed that the chief engineer suggested we add ultrasonic inspection to the fan disc program.

He reminded me we had already asked the airlines to accelerate their compressor spool program and, if we added the extra fan disc inspection, it would put a heavy burden on the airline shops. He also said that neither the procedure nor the tooling had been developed to inspect fan discs, adding that we never had a problem with a fan disc and they were fully inspectable using the FPI process.

Following that call, I did one thing and did not do another: I accepted his argument and did not call the chief engineer to let him know we would not be following his suggestion. I would come to regret both decisions.

Let's step back a moment and revisit what was known during the time period from 1983 to 1989, before the UA 232 disaster:

1. On rare occasions, the titanium melting process produced hard alpha defects, which escaped the inspection processes used at manufacture.
2. There were no events that resulted in an unsafe landing.
3. There were no defects or cracks found on fan discs.
4. It was possible to visually inspect fan discs during the FPI process, but more difficult with compressor spools.

5. Hard alpha defects had to be cracked or voided to be detected by either of the inspection processes used.
6. Engine running and stress produce the cracks in hard alpha, making it more detectable.
7. FPI, a visual process, was vulnerable to "human factors and could only detect cracks that were on the surface."

And here's what we did:

1. Inspected as many parts as possible in the overhaul shops.
2. Used both FPI and immersion ultrasonic techniques on the parts that were hard to visually inspect. (Fan discs were capable of being visually inspected without the use of a mirror.)
3. Put a long-term plan in place to eliminate the problem.

What we failed to recognize and to address was the vulnerability in the FPI process due to human error. As fate would have it, about one year prior to the accident, the fan disc that would eventually initiate the UA 232 event was in the United Airlines' shop where it was FPI inspected. No defects or cracks were found, and it was returned to service.

When the NTSB examined the disc fragments after the accident, they found evidence that at the time of that inspection, there was a crack about one-half-inch long on the surface of the disc in one of the highest stress areas of the part. A crack propagation analysis correlated well with that finding, leading the NTSB to conclude that the FPI inspection that was done one year before the accident had missed the crack!

Their investigation into that inspection process did not reveal any problems. It was done properly and in compliance with the approved procedures. The only conclusion that could be drawn from that was the inspector, for unknown reasons, missed the crack. A "human factor." But that missed vulnerability allowed the chain of events to go unbroken one last time.

I couldn't help but ask myself if I was one of the many people involved that failed to break the chain? I kept thinking about the chief engineer's suggestion to ultrasonically inspect fan discs as well as spools. Would that added inspection have detected the crack? Why did I decide to accept the product support manager's argument to not do that? Should I have brought that decision to others in the organization to see if they thought it was the right thing to do? Why didn't the chief engineer follow up on his recommendation? I had many questions; they haunted me.

However, the reality was that between 1971 (when the titanium was melted) and 1989 (when the accident happened), there were numerous chances for the chain of events to be broken. I was one of a number of people who had an opportunity to break the chain but didn't. So, my personal goal became trying to understand why. I thought about it for several years following the accident, especially the things that stood out:

1. There were numerous areas in the titanium melting and inspection processes where there were vulnerabilities. They were known to the people who were deeply immersed in the details of the processes. They addressed them as part of "doing

their job," but did not raise them up to those in the organization who had the overall responsibility for the business, its products, or its customers. I will use the term "logo." This left the logos vulnerable to the risks involved. Once again, a "forest from the trees" perspective.

2. The level of risk was underestimated at every level and by every organization. Yes, there were problems, but they were being worked. No, there had never been a fatal accident due to the hard alpha issue. The FPI process was the way inspections were done in the overhaul shops and the industry standard. Yes, the three hydraulic lines were close together in the tail of the airplane, but the chances of them all being hit was judged to be "remote."

3. Relative to what I personally did, there were two things that rise to top of mind: First was agreeing with the plan to not ultrasonically inspect fan discs; second was not going back to the chief engineer to tell him about that plan. I made those decisions on my own.

4. Organizational complexity was a factor. The aircraft manufacturer was aware that the hydraulic lines were close together, but the engine manufacturer was not. The chief engineer suggested we should ultrasonically inspect fan discs, but left it to others to actually ensure the inspection took place.

5. Measurements and culture played roles as well. Take, for example, the response of the product support manager when I asked him to introduce a new inspection. He did not want to burden his customers because he was measured on keeping

them happy. I wanted to do that, also, because I sensed that supporting the customer was a fundamental part of our corporate culture.

I had all of this in mind, but was unsure what to do about it. Then, late in 1995, I was given the opportunity to be the chief engineer of GE Aircraft Engines. Along with the promotion came the responsibility for managing the Flight Safety Office, an organization that advised our company on safety matters and investigated accidents when there was engine involvement. I felt like this was my opportunity to address some of the lessons learned from the UA 232 experience.

To do this, I thought that whatever process we adopted, it would have to do several things: define an easy way for employees to raise potential safety issues up to the logo, avoid individuals making critical decisions on their own without leveraging the best intellect and knowledge of the logo, influence the cultural sensitivity of the organization to assure that all "felt" that product safety was the underlying value for the logo, and assure that appropriate levels of the organization were involved in making decisions that could potentially threaten the entire organization.

In simple terms, I wanted to make it easy for issues to be raised and put decision-making power in the hands of those who had responsibility for the product and the resources to address them. And, it was important to ensure the logo had oversight and responsibility for decisions, plans and execution of those plans. The overall goal was to get issues raised and addressed and then have the organization's best resources focused on solving them.

However, when we tried to formulate a formal company policy to do all of that, we ran into questions: What is a safety issue? How can we make decisions that reflect the best thinking of the whole organization? How might we create an environment where employees can bring up potential safety issues without fear of repercussions? How should the resources needed to run a critical safety program be managed?

Needless to say, this was quite a learning experience.

Eventually, the difficulties were overcome and a formal company policy was implemented which addressed the issues I felt were important learnings from the UA 232 event. This policy has since been updated and improved and is still in use today.

Chapter 9
Principles

Principles: *A fundamental truth or proposition that serves as the foundation for a system of belief or behavior or for a chain of reasoning.*

In the years following the UA 232 accident, I kept thinking about the role that I played and what we at GE engines could have done better. That led to a set of principles which we eventually used as the basis for a company policy aimed at improving the way we uncovered and addressed product safety issues. I also planned to use those principles as a basis for writing this book. But, when I got into the Flint, Michigan, and VW events, it became obvious they were far different than UA 232. I was struck by what seemed to be a total disregard for the value ethical behavior. Because of that, I knew it had to be included in whatever set of principles I would propose.

My goal is to define what I believe are the things an organization must do to reduce the probability of experiencing a doomsday event. You will note that I said reduce the probability, not eliminate, because that is simply not realistic. I will say, however, that if these principles are adhered to, the consequences of such events will be far less onerous.

At the highest level, the intent of the principles is to: (1) create an environment where all in the organization recognize a responsibility to place the welfare of the user and the organization above their own; (2) define a process that leads to decisions that reflect that responsibility; and (3) allows the responsible party (the logo) to make the final decision.

Let's start with the principle of values:

Clearly communicate the values of the enterprise

This principle is closely related to the "elephants," safety and ethical behavior, discussed earlier in the book. If product safety and ethical behavior are communicated by management as fundamental values, everyone in the organization will use them as a basis to make decisions. It is a way of counteracting the influences of the goals and measurement factors that employees are faced with every day.

Another advantage of adhering to this principle is that everyone will be cognizant of the fact that not only the "what" but the "how" they do their jobs is vitally important. Employees will feel good about what they are doing and recognize that their work is important to the enterprise.

The second principle relates to culture:

Build and nurture the "right" culture

Culture is how any organization adheres to the perceived values of the enterprise and that has a direct influence on how employees do their job. But what is the right culture?

Every enterprise must be built on a foundation of ethical actions. There is simply no compromise on this principle if any organization wants to remain in business. Later, when you look at the examples, you will notice the consequences for events based on unethical behavior are much more severe than those associated with product safety.

People may forgive you for making a mistake, but they will not forgive you if you cheat. Further, ethics-based events can have serious consequences for the individual employees involved, as well as the organization itself. In both the Flint lead-tainted water doomsday event and the VW emissions scandal, criminal charges have already been filed with more to follow.

Another characteristic of the right culture is that it is open. An open culture means an organization's management makes it clear they want to hear about issues that arise. An open culture exists only when everyone's opinion is respected. Employees' input is heard and considered seriously by management. And management's decisions are accepted and seen through the lens that the issue was given fair consideration. Basically, the right culture is one where ethical behavior is the way business is done and the atmosphere is such that there are open lines of communication from the bottom of the organization to the top, and vice versa. The right values and culture become the very foundation of any process aimed at avoiding doomsday events. Without them, you have nothing.

The next principle addresses what I believe to be the single most important lesson learned from the UA 232 doomsday event:

Always get diverse input when making critical decisions

I decided it was OK to not add an inspection for fan discs. Compressor spools were being inspected using two methods. The fan discs were made from titanium, just like the spools. There were four previous failures of titanium spools. However, I fell into the trap of believing that since there were no fan disc failures, and fan discs were visually inspectable, that it would be OK. My perception of the risk was obviously different than the chief engineer's. That let the organizational culture factor of supporting the customer lead me to making the decision. Had I gone back to the chief engineer or involved other knowledgeable people in that decision process, the result might have been different

By looking at these—and other events throughout the years—I've concluded that when making any important decision, it is mandatory to seek out the opinions of those whose perspective is different from our own and are not influenced by the same goals, measurements, and perceptions of risk. They should also have a technical understanding of the issues involved. I did the right thing when I went to the chief engineer before the UA 232 event. He was technically astute. He grasped the risk involved and was not influenced by the same decision factors as I was. His view of the risks was also much broader than mine, and his perception told him that the pain of having to do fan disc inspections was far outweighed by the risk of another failure. In addition, he was not encumbered by the same parochial measurements the product support manager or I had. In effect, he was free to think outside of the box. But why then did the chain of events not get broken? That brings us to the next principle:

Trust but verify

It didn't get broken because the chief engineer did not follow up on his recommendation. He trusted me to get the inspections done, but did not verify that I did them. Between the two of us, we lost an opportunity to potentially prevent the accident. It is critical to verify that the intent of every decision and every plan is fully executed. There are always many reasons why plans are not fulfilled. Will there be hardware available? Will the customers do what we have asked them to do? How quickly will all the equipment be modified? Will the regulatory agencies accept the plan? It takes a disciplined and sustained effort to assure that all the hurdles to completion are cleared.

The important lesson from this is that it is critical to verify that the plan is being carried out as intended. I might even suggest that, should the worst occur, a plan not executed is worse than no plan at all.

The next principle is one that relates to whom will be responsible should a doomsday event occur?

The logo is responsible so the logo should make the decision

The dictionary defines *"responsible"* as *"the state or fact of being answerable, or accountable for something **within one's power to control or manage.**"*

Note the underlined words: within one's power to control or manage. In the context of doomsday events, this is the organization or person who has the resources and power to fix a problem. There's a much simpler way to define who is responsible: The responsible party is the one who gets the blame and suffers the consequences. And, in the case of doomsday events, it is always the organization or the logo. You saw this in the UA 232 case with GE, United Airlines, and McDonnell Douglas. You will also see it again when we go through the BP, GM and VW events. In cases where governments are involved, there is still blame, but the consequences are a bit different. In those cases, the consequences are political. Unfortunately, the financial consequences from those events fall to the taxpayer.

The reality is that it is impossible for an organization to unilaterally delegate away their responsibility. The responsible organization does not get to choose who gets blamed. Rather, the outside world does.

Those who have the power to control and the responsibility for the actions of the enterprise should have the final say in the decisions that control its future. Clearly, that means the very upper management of the organization. There are two things that are required to do that: they must know the issue exists; and they must be well informed. This is where the foundation principles of values, culture, and diverse input come into play. Without them, it is nearly impossible to uncover serious threats to the organization and to take actions to mitigate them. Upper management must constantly communicate the values of product safety and ethical behavior. They must make it known to everyone that they **want to know** about potential issues. Once those issues are raised, they must have an established and disciplined process to evaluate those issues and determine what to do about them. This brings us to the next principle:

Define individual and organizational roles and responsibilities

Whatever process the organization adopts to manage product safety or ethics issues, there must be a formal set of policies and procedures that defines everyone's responsibilities, as well as the organizational structure to carry it out. Without that institutionalized framework, the process will descend into chaos.

Good product safety and ethics policies should address the organizational structure, assign responsibilities, and define who must be involved in the decision process.

In addition, the responsibility of every individual in the organization to report issues and concerns should be specifically spelled out along with a detailed process of how to do it. These policies should also address how an employee would be protected should they fear retaliation for reporting a concern.

In the case of product safety, there is one more thing that such a policy should address: how and when it is appropriate to quantify the level of risk. The reason is that quantifying risk is exceptionally difficult and depends on the data that is available. The policy should make it clear that appropriate approval is required and that the analysis methodology be clearly documented.

Whatever the process, it must be well defined and everyone must understand how it works and what their responsibilities are.

Several other points: It is not realistic to expect any organization's upper management to be deeply involved in identifying and deciding on every single concern that is raised. There must be a working-level process where issues can be raised, evaluated for their criticality, and mitigation plans developed. These decisions and plans then should be brought to upper management for review and concurrence. That assures decisions and plans make sense, reflect the values and needs of the overall enterprise, and have been based on a diversity of inputs. The logo will be responsible for the mess, regardless of the cause, so it is only fitting the management of the logo be directly involved in making critical decisions and shoulder their responsibility for the outcome.

One last point regarding policies, procedures and processes—the principle of trust but verify applies as well. You cannot afford to assume they will be carried out as envisioned. There must be a follow-up effort that tracks how it they are working and adjusts to compensate for issues that have come up.

At GE Aircraft Engines, we had a member of the flight safety office participate in the meetings of the organizations that were responsible for making decisions related to product safety. Their role in those meetings was to be not only a participant but an observer of how the process was working: Were the appropriate attendees present? Did the meetings occur on the defined schedule? Was the environment conducive to identifying issues?

The good news about doomsday events is that they happen very infrequently. The bad news is that the threat of complacency is real. If left alone, any process will decay into being an exercise in bureaucracy.

In summary, the principles are:

- **Clearly communicate the values of the enterprise.**

- **Build and nurture the "right" culture.**

- **Always get diverse input when making critical decisions.**

- **Trust but verify.**

- **The logo is responsible so the logo should make the decision.**

- **Define individual and organizational roles and responsibilities.**

Now let's look at several other recent doomsday events to see which factors were influential in the decision process leading up to them and if the above principles apply.

Chapter 10
A Good "Bad" Example – BP Oil Spill

Before we delve into these "bad" example events, it's worth admitting I have no direct knowledge of what happened behind the scenes with any of them. Let's assume, however, that what was reported in the media is what really happened, and the information reported during subsequent investigations into each is factual.

The purpose here is to analyze how each of these recent events unfolded, review the decision-making process that led up to the respective doomsday events, and then identify which factors were most influential in causing the problem and which of the principles apply.

In March 2008, BP purchased the rights to drill at a site in the Gulf of Mexico, approximately 40 miles off the coast of Louisiana, called the Macondo Prospect. It partnered with—and chartered—Transocean Ltd., to provide a semi-submersible platform that would be used to drill the well. BP served as the operator and principal developer of the Macondo Well, owning a 65 percent share of the project. Twenty-five percent was owned by Anadarko Petroleum Corp.; the remaining 10 percent was owned by MOEX Offshore.

The platform where the project would be eventually be launched from was going to be used to drill a deep well—18,360 feet below sea level in approximately 5,100 feet of water. The plan was to drill the well and then cap it so the oil could be extracted at a later time. BP contracted with Halliburton to cap the well.

With this group of players in place, the stage was set for a highly complex and technically challenging project. BP maintained overall responsibility for the initiative, but both Transocean and Halliburton would play key roles due to their respective areas of expertise. By looking at a timeline of events, we can get a better sense of what happened, as well as the factors that influenced the decision-making process.

2009

February: BP files an impact plan which states it is "unlikely that an accidental surface or subsurface oil spill would occur from the proposed activities." In the event an accident did take place, the plan explained that because the well was 48 miles from shore and due to the response capabilities that would be implemented, no significant adverse impacts would be expected.

Analysis: *Note the apparent perception of low risk.*

April 6: The U.S. Department of the Interior exempts BP from a detailed environmental impact study after concluding that a massive oil spill was unlikely.

Analysis: *Another perception of low risk, this time on the part of the regulator.*

June 22: A BP senior drilling engineer warns that the metal casing for the blowout preventer might collapse under high pressure.

Analysis: *A technical expert inside the organization identified a risk and voiced a concern. Was this risk properly considered by the BP organization? Did the engineer feel as if he could effectively voice this concern to his upper management? What was the BP culture at the time? Was there a process in place that allowed employees to report safety concerns to management?*

October 7: Transocean Marianas semi-submersible rig begins drilling the well.

November 9: Hurricane Ida damages the Transocean Marianas rig badly enough that it must be replaced with a new rig. This new rig is named "Deepwater Horizon."

2010

February 15: The Deepwater Horizon rig begins drilling the Macondo well with a target completion date of March 8 at a total budgeted cost of $96 million.

Analysis: *This becomes part of the company's goals and measurements.*

March: An accident onboard the Deepwater Horizon damages a gasket on the rig's blowout preventer.

Analysis: *A warning that there were unknown risks.*

April 1: A Halliburton employee warns that BP's use of cement "was against our best practices."

Analysis: *An instance of an expert from the company that had to do the actual work whose warnings fell on the deaf ears. Why did this occur? Potentially because he was not a BP employee. Did he warn Halliburton management? Did Halliburton warn BP at the right level? Whose responsibility was it to react? Is Halliburton responsible, too, for not taking action itself?*

April 6: The Minerals Management Service (MMS) issues a permit for the well with the following notation: "Exercise caution while drilling due to indications of shallow gas and possible water flow."

Analysis: *Another warning.*

April 9: BP drills the last section with the wellbore 18,360 feet below sea level, but the last 1,192 feet need casing. Halliburton recommends a liner/tieback casing that will provide four redundant barriers against potential flow. Instead, BP decides to proceed with a single liner that provides fewer barriers and is faster to install and less expensive—$7 million versus $10 million.

Analysis: *BP's decision to meet goals and measurements overwhelms its perception of potential risk. This occurs despite the expert contractor's warning. It also serves as the second time Halliburton did not escalate its warning to BP nor choose to refuse to move forward with the project in spite of the inherent risks. It begs the question of whether Halliburton was concerned about the impact on its measurements and/or future business opportunities with BP.*

April 14: A BP drilling engineer emails a colleague: "This has been a nightmare well which has everyone all over the place."

Analysis: *This is a prime example of the importance of clear communication and the use of prudent language, which will be discussed in later chapters.*

April 15: The same BP drilling engineer informs a Halliburton executive that BP plans to use six centralizers when the Halliburton recommendation is 21 centralizers. The BP engineer replies in an email: "It's too late to get more product on the rig; our only option is to rearrange placement of the centralizers." Halliburton also recommends circulating the drilling mud from the bottom of the well all the way up to the surface to remove air pockets and debris which can contaminate the cement, saying in an email, "At least circulate one bottoms up on the well before doing a cement job." Despite this recommendation, BP cycles only 261 barrels of mud, a fraction of the total mud used in the well.

Analysis: *Again, BP disregards the advice of experts in an attempt to meet measurements. Halliburton does not take a stand, despite its warnings. Should there have been an escalation process defined between the companies at the contractual level to address potential safety issues like this? Should the contractor have any responsibility for the outcome as it has expressed real concerns about BP's actions?*

April 15: MMS approves an amended permit for BP to use a single liner with fewer barriers.

Analysis: *Regulatory agency did not properly assess the risk. Was this a case of "it never happened before" or could* *the technical competency of the agency vis-a-vis that of the contractor be questioned?*

April 16: BP's operations drilling engineer emails the BP drilling engineer (from above), confirming the six centralizer approach, saying six should be adequate to obtain a proper seal in the well: "Who cares, it is done, end of story, will probably be fine and we'll get a good cement job." *(according to a copy of the email cited in court papers)*

   Analysis: *Note the perception of risk and the tone of the language used. The "safety elephant" does not appear to be heard.*

April 17: Deepwater Horizon completes its drilling. The well is prepared to be cemented so that another rig can later retrieve the oil. The blowout preventer is tested and found "functional." A Halliburton executive reports (I assume to BP) that using only six centralizers "would likely produce channeling and a failure of the cement job."

April 18: A Halliburton executive's report says the "well is considered to have a gas flow problem." Another contractor, Schlumberger, flies a crew to the rig to conduct a cement bond log in order to determine whether the cement has bonded to the casing and its surrounding formations—as required in the rules.

April 19: Halliburton completes cementing the final string and determines its project is finished.

April 20: The doomsday event occurs …

7 a.m.: BP cancels a recommended cement bond test. Conducting the test would have taken between nine and 12 hours and cost $128,000. By cancelling the cement test, BP paid only $10,000.

Analysis: *This is yet another example of measurements and perception of risk.*

11:15 a.m.: The Schlumberger crew leaves on an 11:15 a.m. helicopter flight. BP officials gather on the platform to celebrate seven years without an injury on the rig. The planned moving of the Deepwater Horizon to another location was 43 days past due and the delay had cost BP $21 million.

Analysis: *Did this influence the decisions made?*

9:49 p.m.: A rig shaking shock occurs with no warning. Magenta warnings began to flash on an employee's monitor screen, indicating the most dangerous level of combustible gas intrusion.

9:56 p.m.: Gas, oil, and concrete from the Deepwater Horizon explode up the wellbore onto the deck and then catch fire. The explosion kills 11 platform workers and injures 17 others; another 98 people survive without physical injury.

After the actual explosion, the various parties involved took a number of other actions which exacerbated the consequences even more. As a result, the flow of oil into the Gulf of Mexico lasted 87 days and created severe environmental problems. BP did not accurately report the flow rate of the oil spill, which led to accusations that the company purposely misled the government and public as to the extent of the problem.

In 2012, BP and the U.S. Department of Justice settled criminal charges against the company: BP pled guilty to 11 counts of manslaughter, two misdemeanors, and one felony count of lying to Congress. The company also agreed to four years of government monitoring of its safety practices and ethics. The Environmental Protection Agency (EPA) announced BP would be temporarily banned from any new contracts with the U.S. government. As of February 2013, criminal and civil payments surrounding the Deepwater Horizon disaster cost BP $42.2 billion.

I will let you make your own assessment about the overall disaster and its impact, but based on my experience, the three most influential factors leading to this event are:

1. An obsession with meeting goals and measurements.
2. A culture of arrogance
3. Organizational complexity and blurred lines of responsibility.

It appears the lack of focus on the value, safety, allowed goals and measurements to overwhelm the perception of risk. It's really the only good explanation for the decisions that were made

I have no way of assessing exactly what the culture inside BP was at the time of the Deepwater Horizon disaster, but it appears that it was one of arrogance: "We know better than anyone else. We know what the risks are. We have done this before."

When you combine arrogance with a "let's get this thing done" culture, it becomes even easier to understand why a series of bad decisions were made.

All of that said, it leads one to look to the leadership of the organizations and question their role in defining and communicating the values of the enterprise and making sure that the people inside their organizations recognized their responsibility to, above all, do business in a manner that reflects those values. Clearly, in this case, the money elephant was heard over the value "elephant", safety.

Organizational structure also made it very difficult to determine who was either responsible or accountable for the decisions. Case in point: During the post-event investigation, a high-level BP manager was asked the question, "Who was responsible?"

His answer: "…. Sometimes contractors manage the risk and sometimes we do. Most of the time it is a team effort."

If you couple this with the additional complication that BP was a customer for both Transocean and Halliburton, it becomes a bit easier to see how difficult it would have been for them to tell the "king that he had no clothes on."

The organizational complexity involved in this event is not a case of complexity within BP but complexity between BP and its contractors. This was highlighted by Halliburton's attempt to tell BP the planned approach to capping the well was wrong. Most large projects involve multiple organizations that play important roles in the eventual outcome of the effort. Despite this, all participating organizations own the same responsibility to ensure product safety and ethical behavior. When you analyze the relationship between BP and Halliburton, it is easy to see that Halliburton would not want to come into conflict with what probably was one of their best customers. However, had there been a process for Halliburton at the highest levels to communicate their concerns to BP at the highest levels, I'm convinced a different decision would have been made. Had BP not addressed Halliburton's concerns, I would submit that Halliburton should have refused to proceed as directed. But neither thing happened. Instead, the explosion and spill occurred.

There are, however, ways to address this. Initially, all contractual arrangements between participants should be written in such a manner as to define a communication procedure where the upper management of the organizations can bring up critical issues and concerns. This would directly address the "decision factor" of organizational complexity and assure the logos have considered the diverse input necessary to make sound decisions.

Looking back, Halliburton suffered significant consequences because they did not convey their concerns to the very top management of BP nor did they refuse to proceed. Did the "Halliburton logo" make the decision or did someone deep inside the organization conclude that "if it is BP's decision, we have to do it their way"? In my opinion, they ceded their right and responsibility to protect the Halliburton logo. In turn, they suffered the consequences.

The scorecard:

Decision Factors that Apply 6 of 6
All of the six factors, values, culture, goals,

measurements, perception of risk, and organizational complexity, were influential in the BP event.

Principles Violated 5 of 6
Had five of the six principles (communicate values, the right culture, get diverse input, logo makes the decision, define roles and responsibilities) been applied, I would speculate that the event would have never happened.

Chapter 11
Another Good "Bad" Example - GM Ignition Switch

The General Motors ignition switch scandal, which evolved throughout more than a decade, is a bit more subtle than the BP oil spill because the "tea leaves" warning of a problem were difficult to read. Because of this, it took significantly longer to diagnose the real problem and respond to it appropriately. That said, GM's slow response— even after it was clear that the problem was a safety issue— transformed it into a doomsday event. As this event does not have the organizational and contractual complexities of BP's Deepwater Horizon disaster, it's easier to simply dive into the timeline and subsequent analysis.

2001

GM engineers experience problems with the mechanism that is supposed to hold the ignition key in place. An internal report indicates the problem was solved by a redesign of the switch.

2003

A GM service technician sees a Saturn Ion stall while it is being driven with several other keys on the key ring. He writes: "The additional weight of the keys had worn out the ignition switch."

The National Highway Traffic Safety Administration (NHTSA) receives the first of many complaints about unexpected shutdowns in the later-recalled models.

2004

A GM engineer bumps the key in a Chevrolet Cobalt during testing, causing it to abruptly lose power.

2005

GM receives additional reports of its Chevrolet Cobalt losing power when accidently bumped or moved out of the "run" position. In response, engineers propose that the head of the key be redesigned so that other things hanging from the keys are less likely to jostle it. This proposal is initially approved, but later cancelled. Internal GM documents say that, among other things, the fix was too costly.

Analysis: *This is a good example of the day-to-day struggle to balance the "money elephant" with the "safety elephant." This is especially true because at this point there was no warning or overt signs that losing power could result in fatalities (perception of risk).*

A "brand quality" division of GM notices a higher rate of buybacks and urges the company to reopen its investigation into the ignition switch issue.

A fatal accident occurs which—as is claimed in a lawsuit—was tied to the ignition switch.

Analysis: *It is not clear from any public filings whether GM drew the same conclusion.*

GM issues a service bulletin alerting consumers and others to the ignition switch problem. The automaker does not issue a recall.

2006

Delphi, the company that manufactures the switch, proposes a design change. A GM engineer signs off on the changes and the new part goes into production. However, the part number is not changed, which makes it unidentifiable from the previous design.

Analysis: *This seems like a small detail, but doing so allows the use of existing inventory—saving time and money. However, it also makes it impossible to know which cars are susceptible to the problem—which will later significantly increase the size of the recall.*

GM dealers hand out "key inserts" to limit key movement to 474 owners of models that will later be recalled.

Analysis: *This is another early warning, but I still do not believe the safety risk was yet apparent to GM.*

2007

GM begins installing redesigned ignition switches on its 2007 model cars.

During an unrelated meeting with auto safety regulators, GM employees are informed of a fatal 2005 Cobalt crash in which airbags did not deploy. By the end of year, GM is aware of 10 deadly Cobalt accidents in which airbags failed.

Analysis: It appears as though GM still had not convinced themselves that the ignition switch was the reason the airbags did not deploy in the accidents. Sometimes, determining root cause is difficult and time consuming. Also at question is whether upper GM management was made aware of these events or if it was left up to those working the issue to recognize the switch as the cause for the non-deployment and set the priority on how the problem should be addressed.

A GM engineer is assigned to look at Cobalt front crashes in which the airbags did not deploy in order to identify common characteristics. In four of the nine crashes, the ignition was not in "run" at the time of impact.

Analysis: If GM as an organization knew about this data, it seems unlikely they only would have assigned one engineer.

An official with the NHTSA pushes to open an investigation after noticing "a pattern of reported (airbag) non-deployments" involving Chevrolet Cobalts and Saturn Ions. This official is blocked by others in the department who don't believe any action is warranted.

Analysis: It would be interesting to know what factors influenced that internal NHTSA decision. It also provides a good example of how different people perceive risk.

2008

A NHTSA contractor tells regulators that a Cobalt fatal crash was related to the ignition switch problem about which GM had notified its dealers.

In response to a complaint, NHTSA writes to a driver of a Chevy HHR that stalled: "At this time there is insufficient evidence to warrant opening a safety defect investigation."

Analysis: *Once again, this response points out that the tie between the switch and the non-deployment was not clear.*

2009

March 29: Rick Wagoner resins as CEO of GM as part of the company's restructuring plans. Frederick "Fritz" Henderson named as new CEO.

Under new leadership, GM looks at "black box" data for 14 crashes and finds that the ignition switch was recorded in the "accessory" position for half of them

June 1: GM files for Chapter 11 bankruptcy protection.

July 10: GM exits bankruptcy.

December 1: Fritz Henderson resigns; Ed Whitacre named new CEO.

December 18: Fatal crash of 2006 Cobalt in Tennessee. Airbags did not deploy.

2010

February: NHTSA office of defects investigation considers Cobalt trend information regarding the non-deployment of airbags. Investigators determine the data does not show a definitive trend and drops probe.

March 10: Brooke Melton is killed on her 29th birthday after her 2005 Chevy Cobalt crashes and its airbags do not deploy. Her parents' subsequent lawsuit will eventually bring the ignition switch problem to the public's attention.

September 1: Daniel Akerson replaces Ed Whitacre as CEO of GM.

2011

A new investigation is opened to look into front crashes of Chevy Cobalts and Pontiac G5s where airbags did not deploy. The ignition switches are removed from cars in salvage yards and tested.

2012

Engineers notice that all the crashes in which the ignition was switched out of "run" only happened in cars from the 2007 model year and earlier.

Analysis: *This is where the link between the pre-redesign ignition switches and the non-deployments was firmly established. The delay in taking action from this point on will significantly increase the consequences for GM.*

2013

GM investigators notice that ignition switches in cars built in later years (than 2007) are less prone to moving out of the "run" position than ignitions in earlier models.

GM hires outside engineers to conduct a thorough assessment of ignition switches from cars made prior to 2007. The engineers conclude that changes were made to the ignition switch sometime after the cars first went into production.

Analysis: *The failure to make the redesigned switch a new part number made the data analysis more difficult because the change could not be identified. Sometimes what seems like an insignificant decision at the time can greatly influence the final result.*

GM's executive field action decision committee is asked to consider a recall of Chevrolet Cobalt and Pontiac G5 cars from the 2007 model year and earlier.
Analysis: *This is the point where the corporation recognizes the problem and decides on an action plan.*

2014

January: GM gets a new CEO, Mary Barra. She replaces Daniel Akerson.

February 7: GM issues a recall of approximately 800,000 Chevrolet Cobalt and Pontiac G5 vehicles.

This recall eventually led to a worldwide recall of more than 2.6 million GM automobiles. Mary Barra, GM's CEO, was called to testify several times before Congress as the death toll kept rising. Eventually, the company took a charge in excess of $1.2 billion. On April 7, 2014, automobile dealers began making repairs on the affected cars. Barra launched an internal investigation at the company as a criminal investigation was independently initiated seeking reasons why the recall was delayed. As of this writing, 15 employees have been dismissed and five others were disciplined for what was deemed a "pattern of incompetence and neglect."

Looking back at the GM ignition switch doomsday event in its entirety, there was a confluence of factors which influenced how the problem was handled.

From about 2001 through 2007, it was not clear how the switch related to the airbags not deploying—despite an inkling the two were related. However, as an engineer, I can only speculate that between 2010 and 2011, investigators inside GM who were working on the problem probably had a strong suspicion that this was the case. They certainly concluded that was the case by 2012. However, this was during the time period when GM was in financial distress and was bailed out by the U.S. government.

Complicating the problem is the revolving door at the CEO position—by 2014, the company had made four different CEO changes. Leadership changes have dramatic impacts on company cultures. That makes it difficult to ascertain who actually is making the decisions that matter. Beyond that, it's hard to understand what resources were available to address the problem. And just as important, what were the company's priorities during this time? Staying solvent certainly had to be at the top of the list. As engineers and investigators weren't completely sure the switch was the actual cause of the issue, there appears to be a "wait and see" attitude at work.

This is, in many respects, a typical situation in larger companies: You know there is a problem, but the level of threat is unknown. GM was not even sure themselves if the switch was the real culprit. The available courses of action are often difficult to undertake and expensive to pursue. Thus, the general inclination among most parties involved is to wait until things become clearer before taking potential solutions to upper management and asking for resources to address the issue.

In retrospect, the only reason the GM ignition switch event became a doomsday event is because of its delay in acting on the problem. I would argue between 2003 and 2012 the company was unsure of what the underlying issue really was. Without that knowledge, determining the level of risk is extremely difficult. However, I would also argue the reason it took so long to connect the dots and to decide on an action plan was that the company was in a state of turmoil. If nothing else, there was a leadership vacuum inside the organization, which made deciding on priorities, staffing levels, and how fast to react to issues much more difficult.

Personally, I believe the most important reason this event occurred is because of how the lack of perceived leadership impacted the culture inside the organization. It almost seems that GM was like a ship without a captain. There was nobody at the helm to assure that the values of the corporation were communicated and appropriate actions taken to meet potential threats. This led to a "business as usual "scenario when they were faced with a problem that was difficult to pin down. Because of that, and the fact that there was not a defined process to do it, the issue was not brought up to the logo level. Without leadership and a well-defined decision process, it is hard for the logo to make timely decisions on issues which potentially have significant consequences.

The scorecard:

Decision Factors that Apply 3 of 6

Of the six factors, I believe that values, culture, and perception of risk were the most influential.

Principles Violated 5 of 6

Five of the six principles would have come into play—communicate values, right culture, logo makes the decision, defined roles and responsibilities, trust but verify.

Chapter 12
A Really Bad Example

Doomsday events such as the BP oil spill and GM ignition switch problems are examples where ultimate responsibility, and therefore the consequences, are clearly borne by the corporations that delivered the product. There is one heinous example of a doomsday event that involves multiple governments and government agencies where, as a result, the ultimate responsibility and therefore the consequences, are borne by all—and regrettably, borne by none.

Flint, Michigan's lead-tainted water disaster demonstrates how singular political goals and a bureaucratic culture can lead people to do things that are irrational, irresponsible, and quite frankly, immoral. It exemplifies the power of the "six factors," and serves as a case study for how applying common sense principles and sound processes can help avoid such egregious doomsday events. Be warned, however, as we break down and analyze the details of what happened, it might very well shake your faith in government's ability to protect you and your family's health and well-being.

For purposes of examining this event, I opted to use the Flint Water Advisory Task Force's final report, commissioned by the governor of the state of Michigan, as a reference point. While there are many other sources of information on this subject, this one is the most comprehensive and least biased. It includes a good description of the event, has a detailed timeline, and offers ample insight into how the different organizations participated and how people inside those organizations were influenced by their environment.

First, let's look at the organizational structure of the entities involved to theoretically see who was supposedly responsible for what:

In 2011, Michigan Gov. Rick Snyder invoked a state law that allowed him to appoint an emergency manager (EM) to oversee the city of Flint, which at the time was in financial crisis and receivership. Under the statute, the EM temporarily supplanted the governing body and chief administrative officer of the local government and assumed control of the city of Flint. This EM, formally the emergency financial manager (EFM), reported to the State Department of the Treasury.

The city of Flint, not the state of Michigan, is responsible for its own water supply and therefore meeting the requirements of the Safe Water Drinking Act (SWDA), a federal statute. Flint is located in Genessee County. The Genessee County Health Department is responsible for all health functions for its residents.

The Genessee County Drain Commission (GCDC) was responsible for building a new water line to deliver Lake Huron water to the Flint Water Treatment Plant. In 2011, Genessee County formed the Karegnondi Water Authority (KWA) to develop a raw water pipeline from Lake Huron to supply it and two other counties (Lapeer and Sanilac), as well as the cities of Flint and Lapeer, with water.

The Michigan Department of Environmental Quality (MDEQ) is responsible for ensuring the city's water treatment plant meets the requirements of the SWDA.

The Office of Drinking Water and Municipal Assistance (ODWMA), within the MDEQ, is responsible for advising the water suppliers about how to meet the SWDA requirements. (Note the dual MDEQ responsibility—adviser on how to meet the law's requirements and to also oversee the water supplier to determine that their advice was complied with.)

The U.S. Environmental Protection Agency (EPA) has the ultimate responsibility for protection of public health and management of environmental risks. However, the EPA delegates its authority to enforce the SWDA to relevant state agencies—in this case, the MDEQ and ODWMA. Under this scenario, the MDEQ/ODWMA is the primacy agency directly responsible for compliance with the federal SWDA. To put it in street language: If they say it is OK, it is OK.

The background of how the current Flint water set-up came to be traces back more than a century. The Flint water system was first organized in 1883 under private ownership and the city purchased the water system in 1903. Before 1967, Flint treated Flint River water at its Water Treatment Plant (WTP). To ensure adequacy and reliability of water supplies, Flint signed a long-term water supply contract in 1967 with the Detroit Water and Sewerage Department (DWSD). The DWSD sourced its water from Lake Huron and, as of January 2017, that water had been treated for corrosion control for more than 20 years. Corrosion control is done to prevent lead from leaching out of old lead pipes that lead to homes and is especially important if the source water has corrosive characteristics.

From 1967 through 2014, the Flint WTP served as an emergency backup to DWSD-supplied water. Because of this, the Flint WTP was not operated on an ongoing day-to-day basis, but rather four times per year to maintain readiness as an emergency backup. The WTP was also upgraded periodically to keep it ready for use as an emergency backup.

DWSD provided water to Flint under a 35-year contract which was signed on December 20, 1965. The initial contract term expired in 2000 and, under terms of the agreement, automatically renewed each year unless it was terminated by either party.

As one of DWSD's wholesale customers, Flint was subject to the terms and rate-setting practices applicable to DWSD's wholesale customer communities. During the final 10 years that Flint received contractual service from DWSD, the average annual increase in water charges to Flint was 6.2 percent.

On April 16, 2013, after a symbolic Flint City Council vote that accompanied the Flint emergency manager's decision, the city joined the Karegnondi Water Authority (KWA), which had been established to develop a raw water supply pipeline from Lake Huron. After being advised of the city of Flint's intent, DWSD notified the city of the termination of its then-current water supply contract terms, effective April 2014. DWSD and the city of Flint, both under emergency management, continued unsuccessfully for the next year to negotiate alternative water supply terms. Although the State of Michigan was in control of both cities (Flint and Detroit) at the time, efforts to arrive at an agreement between the parties during the final year of service to the city of Flint ultimately failed.

In April 2014, the city of Flint began treating Flint River water at the Flint WTP on a full-time basis and distributing the treated water to its customers. A critical element of that treatment—corrosion control, as required under EPA's Lead and Copper Rule (LCR)—was incorrectly determined by MDEQ not to be required immediately. Instead, the MDEQ determined that Flint could complete two six-month monitoring periods and then it would then determine whether corrosion control was necessary or not. This was done despite the fact that Flint River water was likely to be significantly more corrosive than the Lake Huron water previously supplied by DWSD!

Shortly after the city began distributing treated water from the Flint WTP, residents began to complain about its odor, taste, and appearance. Numerous water quality problems and operational challenges resulted in water quality violations related to *E. coli* contamination and disinfection by-products (total trihalomethanes or TTHMs).

Ultimately, the corrosiveness of the drinking water leached lead from pipes and plumbing fixtures, and it may have also increased the likelihood of water contamination with Legionella.

At this point, it's also useful to look at the task force's executive Summary, which serves as a good assessment of what happened and a detailed timeline of the events as they took place.

Flint Water Advisory Task Force Final Report
Executive Summary

Summary Statement

  The Flint water crisis is a story of government failure, intransigence, unpreparedness, delay, inaction, and environmental injustice. The Michigan Department of Environmental Quality (MDEQ) failed in its fundamental responsibility to effectively enforce drinking water regulations. The Michigan Department of Health and Human Services (MDHHS) failed to adequately and promptly act to protect public health. Both agencies, but principally the MDEQ, stubbornly worked to discredit and dismiss others' attempts to bring the issues of unsafe water, lead contamination, and increased cases of Legionellosis (Legionnaires' disease) to light. With the city of Flint under emergency management, the Flint Water Department rushed unprepared into full-time operation of the Flint Water Treatment Plant, drawing water from a highly corrosive source without the use of corrosion control. Though MDEQ was delegated primacy (authority to enforce federal law), the United States Environmental Protection Agency (EPA) delayed enforcement of the Safe Drinking Water Act (SDWA) and Lead and Copper Rule (LCR), thereby prolonging the calamity. Neither the governor nor the governor's office took steps to reverse poor decisions by MDEQ and state-appointed emergency managers until October 2015, in spite of mounting problems and suggestions to do so by senior staff members in the governor's office, in part because of continued reassurances from MDEQ that the water was safe. The significant consequences of these failures for Flint will be long-lasting. They have deeply affected Flint's public health, its economic future, and residents' trust in government.

The Flint water crisis occurred when state-appointed emergency managers replaced local representative decision-making in Flint, removing the checks and balances and public accountability that come with public decision-making. Emergency managers made key decisions that contributed to the crisis, from the use of the Flint River to delays in reconnecting to DWSD once water quality problems were encountered. Given the demographics of Flint, the implications for environmental injustice cannot be ignored or dismissed.

The Flint water crisis is also a story, however, of something that did work: the critical role played by engaged Flint citizens, by individuals both inside and outside of government who had the expertise and willingness to question and challenge government leadership, and by members of free press who used the tools that enable investigative journalism. Without their courage and persistence, this crisis likely never would have been brought to light and mitigation efforts never begun.

A Series of Government Failures

Flint water customers were needlessly and tragically exposed to toxic levels of lead and other hazards through the mismanagement of their drinking water supply. The specific events that led to the water quality debacle, lead exposure, heightened Legionella susceptibility, and infrastructure damage are a litany of questionable decisions and failures related to several issues and events, including, but not limited to:

93

• Decisions related to the use of the Flint River as an interim water supply source.

• Inadequate preparation (for example, staffing, training and plant upgrades) for the switch to full-time use of the Flint Water Treatment Plant using the Flint River as the primary water supply source.

• Inadequate and improper sampling of distribution system water quality, potentially in violation of the Safe Drinking Water Act.

• Intransigent disregard of compelling evidence of water quality problems and associated health effects.

• Callous and dismissive responses to citizens' expressed concerns.

• Persistent delays in coordinating appropriate responses to the resultant public health crises once irrefutable evidence of exposure and poisoning was presented.

We cannot begin to explain and learn from these events—our charge—without also highlighting that the framework for this decision-making was Michigan's Emergency Manager Law. This law replaces the decision-making authority of locally elected officials with that of a state-appointed emergency manager. While one must acknowledge that emergency management is a mechanism to address severe financial distress, it is important to emphasize that the role of the emergency manager in Flint places accountability for what happened with state government. Our complete findings and recommendations are provided throughout this report and also are summarized at the close of this Executive Summary. They are formulated to offer specific measures to better safeguard public health, enhance critical water system infrastructure, improve governmental decision-making and regulatory oversight, and mitigate the many negative health and economic effects facing the people of Flint. We hope that our findings and recommendations serve as a guide and template for remediation and recovery in Flint, and for safeguarding the health and well-being of residents across our state.

As you read through the following timeline of what happened in Flint, ask yourselves the following 10 questions:

1. Did the convoluted organizational structure blur the lines of responsibility?
2. What values were communicated by the State of Michigan? Did they reflect concern for safety of the citizens? Did they emphasize doing business ethically?
3. What were the cultures of the respective agencies?
4. Was the goal safe water or something else?
5. Was there adequate oversight in the decision-making process?
6. Did the decisions make sense?
7. What motivated them to not treat the water?
8. Did the agencies make it easy for employees to raise issues as they came to light?
9. What were the ultimate consequences of the decisions that were made?
10. Were the residents themselves responsible for the lead-tainted water because their homes contained lead pipes?

As you consider the answers, try to relate them to the six influence factors: values, goals, culture, organizational complexity, measurements, and perception of risk. How do each of the six play into what happened? Admittedly, this timeline is a bit lengthy and extremely detailed. As you review it, you may find yourself, like me, embroiled in the plot. It reads like a TV soap opera: filled with deceit, recrimination, threats, and outright immoral behavior.

Here is a key to abbreviations used throughout the remainder of this chapter:

Flint Michigan Abbreviations

AL	Action level
CCT	Corrosion control treatment
DWSD	Detroit Water and Sewer Department
DPB	Disinfection by-products
DPW	Department of Public Works
GCDC	Genessee County Drain Commission
GCHD	Genessee County Health Department
EFM	Emergency Financial Manager
EM	Emergency Manager
EPA	Environmental Protection Agency
KWA	Karegnondi Water Authority
LCR	Lead and copper rule
MDEQ	Michigan Department of Environmental Quality
MDHHS	Michigan Department of Health and Human Services
OCCT	Optimum corrosion control treatment
ODWMA	Office of Drinking Water and Municipal Assistance
SWDA	Safe Water Drinking Act
TTHM	Total trihalomethanes
WTP	Water Treatment Plant

Timeline for the Flint, Michigan, lead-tainted water crisis

1947 to 1955

Flint makes improvements to its water treatment plant. Polyphosphate is added to water in small amounts to lesson corrosion of water pipes when they come into contact with cold water.

Analysis: *This was long before Flint got water from DWSD, but it is clear that even back then the issue was recognized as a potential problem.*

1991

The Environmental Protection Agency (EPA) issues the "Lead and Copper Rule" (LCR), which limits the amount of lead and copper allowed to be present in drinking water. The LCR has a goal of zero lead contaminants but sets a limit of 15 parts-per-billion (PPB). It also sets a requirement to implement "optimum corrosion control treatment" (OCCT). However, the definition of OCCT is left up to the primacy agency in charge of monitoring water treatment, in this case the MDEQ-ODWMA.

2002

May 22: Michigan Gov. John Engler invokes the state's fiscal distress statute and declares a financial emergency in Flint, which has a $30 million deficit.

July 8: Engler appoints an Emergency Financial Manager (EFM), Ed Kurtz, a Flint resident and the outgoing Baker College system CEO. Kurtz's term is to last until 2004.

2004

An assessment of Flint River water raises concerns about using it for drinking water due to potential contamination. The state's EFM takeover effectively ends in June.

2006

The Genessee County Drain Commission (GCDC) indicates that Flint River water can be safely treated, but they do not have adequate capacity (enough water to be the sole supplier) for permanent use.

Analysis: *A lot of the discussion during this time period was not about lead contamination but rather about other issues with the water. Lead seems to have been an "elephant," and therefore not a significant part of the conversation—even though the SWDA-LCR clearly put limits on lead and it was known to all parties involved that corrosive water had to be treated to avoid leaching lead from the pipes.*

2010

DWSD and GCDC meet to negotiate the water supply contract. DWSD informs GCDC that upon termination of the contract, DWSD will not continue to provide water to Flint.

2011

July 1: A report is completed for the city of Flint on the feasibility of using the Flint Water Treatment Plant with Flint River as the city's primary water supply. It notes that Flint River water would require more treatment than Lake Huron water and recommends capital improvements. The report also projects capital and operating costs, which include phosphate addition. Phosphate is used to mitigate the corrosive effects of water on pipes.

November 8: The state of Michigan's financial review team recommends the city of Flint once again be placed under the control of an emergency manager.

November 29: Gov. Rick Snyder places Flint in receivership and names Flint's temporary Mayor Michael Brown as its new emergency manager.

December 1: Brown takes office and begins to implement a series of financial reforms to cut costs.

2012

May 9: Flint Department of Public Works (DPW) Director Howard Croft, whose organization is responsible for the water treatment plant, informs District Engineer Michael Prysby of MDEQ Office of Drinking Water and Municipal Assistance (ODWMA) of the city's intent to move forward with the project to eventually get its water from Lake Huron through the KWA.

June 26: Brown sends a letter to the DWSD requesting permission to begin blending Flint River water with treated water from the DWSD. The letter indicates that MDEQ is supporting this option, which would save the city of Flint between $2 million and $3 million annually.

August 8: Gov. Snyder names Ed Kurtz, Flint's EFM from 2002 to 2004, to be the city's new emergency manager. Kurtz appoints Brown, his immediate predecessor, to serve as Flint city administrator.

October 31: The city's analysis finance director suggests the annual cost to purchase water from the DWSD will steadily increase each year to $23 million per year by 2020.

November 6: Flint EM Kurtz sends a letter to the state treasurer indicating that a proposal from DWSD is expected, but that the initial assessment shows switching to KWA is in the city of Flint's best interests.

Analysis: *The EM, who has no technical knowledge regarding water supplies, depends solely on the MDEQ/ODWMA for an assessment of risk. It is not clear if there was any communication between the offices.*

2013

January 23: MDEQ/ODWMA district engineer Prysby emails the head of ODWMA and others about the feasibility of using Flint River water. He cites concerns for utilizing 100 percent Flint River water for the following reasons: need to soften, the potential for more advanced treatment, available capacity and residuals management (disposal of sludge).

Analysis: *Note the apparent silence on lead.*

March 25: Flint City Council votes to approve using KWA pipeline project water. This is the Lake Huron water that will later be available through the to-be-built pipeline. The vote is non-binding since all financial decisions are made by the state treasurer, as advised by the Flint EM.

March 26: Stephen Busch, of MDEQ, emails director Dan Wyant and others warning about Flint River water quality, as well as microbial and disinfection by-product (DPB) risks.

March 27: MDEQ Chief Deputy Director Jim Sygo emails Busch about the Flint River water switch. It reads, in part: *"As you might guess, we are in a situation with emergency financial managers so it's entirely possible that they will be making decisions relative to cost."*

April 15: An analysis undertaken by the EM, MDEQ, and the state-Treasurer's Office of Financial Responsibility independently conclude that the KWA option is less expensive than the current situation.

April 16: Kurtz signs an agreement with KWA and informs the state treasurer.

April 17: The DWSD transmits a letter to Kurtz terminating service, effective April 17, 2014.

May 29: Kurtz sends Gov. Snyder his resignation letter, effective July 3, 2013.

June 13: The city of Flint decides to use Flint River water as a water source.

June 26: Kurtz signs a resolution to hire a consulting firm to prepare the Flint Water Treatment Plant (WTP) for full-time operation, using Flint River water as a source.

> Flint notifies the MDEQ of its intent to use Flint WTP full-time and to use Flint River water for drinking water.
> Flint City Administrator Ed Brown is reappointed as the city's EM.

> Groundbreaking for a new pipeline begins.

July: The city of Flint begins a test to see if WTP could adequately supply water.

Analysis: *Apparently, they just considered flow rate not chemical properties as part of the test as no data exists in the public forum to demonstrate otherwise.*

September: Brown resigns as EM, effective October 31, 2013. Darnell Earley is appointed the new EM.

2014

March 7: Earley sends a letter to the Detroit Department of Sewerage and Water (DWSD) explaining that the city of Flint has made plans to supply its own water and will not accept Detroit's offer to supply water through its services.

March 26: MDEQ district supervisor Busch sends emails to his staff, Liane Shekter-Smith and Richard Benzie, regarding uncertainty on startup requirements for Flint WTP. It reads, in part: *"I would like to make sure everyone is on the same page on ... what Flint will be required to do in order to start using their plant full-time ... starting up for continuous operation will carry significant changes in regulatory requirements so there is a very gray area as to what we consider startup." –Memorandum by EPA director, Office of Ground Water and Drinking Water, November 3, 2015.*

Analysis: *The reason for this uncertainty is that this apparently is the first time since the SWDA was enacted that a city started up their own facility with a new source of raw water.*

April 9: The MDEQ issues permits for WTP enhancements for full-time use.

April 16: Mike Glasgow, Flint WTP laboratory and water quality supervisor, emails the MDEQ requesting information: *"I am expecting changes to our water quality monitoring parameters, and possibly our disinfection or lead and copper monitoring plan .... Any information would be appreciated, because it looks as if we will be starting the plant up tomorrow and are being pushed to start distributing water as soon as possible."*

April 17: Glasgow emails several people at the MDEQ— Adam Rosenthal, Prysby, and Busch, all of whom will later be indicted for their parts in the lead-tainted water crisis. Glasgow's email reads: *"... if water is to be distributed from this plant in the next couple of weeks, it will be against my direction. I need time to adequately train additional staff and to update our monitoring plans before I will feel we are ready. I will reiterate this to management above me, but they seem to have their own agenda."*

April 17: Water service from DWSD officially ends. The city of Flint also conducts two separate public forums regarding the use of Flint River water, upgrades to the city's WTP, and overall cost to switch to KWA.

Let's pause here and review what has transpired to date relative to the city of Flint supplying its own water.

First, Flint officials concluded they could save money by supplying their own water. Next, the DSWD would no longer supply treated water to Flint beyond April 17, 2014, which required Flint to use Flint River water as a source until the KWA pipeline project could deliver Lake Huron water to the city. And third, the MDEQ-ODWMA had not explicitly advised Flint WTP regarding what was required to meet the SWDA-LCR. Pay close attention to the fact that they were looking only at what was "required" to meet the law's requirements, rather than looking at whether the water itself was safe to drink.

Beyond this, the MDEQ-ODWMA knew there were many homes in Flint that had lead service lines and that Flint River water was more corrosive than the Lake Huron water that DWSD had been supplying. They also knew that DWSD had been treating their water for corrosion. And, they knew the detrimental effects of lead were irreversible and children were the most seriously affected.

With all of this in mind, the MDEQ-ODWMA

advised the Flint WTP that corrosion control would **not be required** at startup and that the SWDA requirements for optimum corrosion control treatment (OCCT) would be met by completing two six-month monitoring periods. At that time, based on the results, a decision would be made regarding whether corrosion control treatment (CCT) would be required. In effect, this became an experiment in how fast the Flint River water would corrode lead pipes and leach lead into the water. This is the point where, in my opinion, the event crosses the morality line … and it gets worse.

April 25: Flint officially switches water sources and hosts a "changeover ceremony."

May 15: An EPA employee emails colleagues about concerns a city resident has made about Flint drinking water. It reads: *"Flint River quality is not great but …. plant is producing water that is currently meeting SWDA standards … his doctor says the rash is from the new drinking water … He has no interest in speaking to MDEQ-ODMWA, he doesn't trust anyone in Michigan government."*

  Analysis: *This is the first real indication of a problem. Instead of taking action, the EPA referred the resident to MDEQ.*

June: Complaints intensify. The Flint WTP boosts its use of lime to address hardness concerns.

June 17: MDEQ's Rosenthal emails Flint WTP manager confirming no orthophosphate monitoring is necessary at Flint WTP because no orthophosphate is being added.

Analysis: *The chemical was not added because of the (incorrect) MDEQ-ODWMA interpretation of the SWDA that it did not require corrosion treatment unless two monitoring period results showed that lead levels exceeded the action limit (AL) of 15 PPB for the 90th percentile sample.*

July 1: Flint begins its first six-month monitoring period for lead and copper in the drinking water.

August 15: Flint issues a boil water advisory and increases chlorine use in its water.

September 5: The city issues another boil water advisory and implements another chlorine increase.

October: The Genessee County Health Department expresses concern for an increased incidence of Legionellosis and its possible connection to the water supply.

October 1: Gov. Snyder requests a briefing from the MDEQ in response to the recent advisories and complaints. The MDEQ blames the boil water advisories on a variety of factors, mostly aging cast iron pipes. There is no mention of lead issues in the briefing.

October 13: General Motors announces it is switching from the Flint water system, citing corrosion concerns. MDEQ's Prysby notes that Flint water chloride levels are "easily within" public health guidelines. He also emails others at the MDEQ, stating chloride levels are not "optimal" but are "satisfactory."

October 14: Gov. Snyder's senior staff recommends going back to DWSD water. However, Flint EM Earley indicates the water problems can be solved and it would be "cost prohibitive" to return to DWSD.

October 21: The Michigan Department of Health and Human Services (MDHHS) emails the Genessee County Health Department (GCHD) about MDEQ's Shekter Smith's concern that Flint water would be publicly linked to Legionellosis outbreak. It reads: *"I told her the Flint water was at this point just a hypothesis."* The GCHD dismisses the risk.

December 31: The first six-month round of lead and copper monitoring ends. Results indicates the 90th percentile level were 6 PPB, within the 15 PPB requirement. But two samples were above the 15 PPB level.

Analysis: *Later scrutiny by the EPA and others revealed significant sampling errors, which led some people to be criminally charged in the matter. If done properly, first monitoring data would have indicated a lead problem at this point.*

2015

January 9: The University of Michigan discovered two locations on campus with elevated lead levels.

Analysis: *This is the second warning of elevated levels of lead-tainted water.*

January 12: MDEQ staff members communicate via email about the deision to provide water coolers at the city of Flint's state office building. Discussions include thoughts about how it will affect residents' perception of drinking water safety, and how the decision will "make it more difficult ... for ODWMA staff."

January 13: Gov. Snyder announces Jerry Ambrose, who had been Flint's finance and administration director, will replace Michael Earley as emergency manager. It represents the sixth change in the EM office.

January 21: MDEQ's Shekter-Smith emails colleagues: "... when Flint decided to ... operate using Flint River water, our role wasn't to tell them our opinion, only what steps would be necessary to make the switch."

February 1: MDEQ's Wurfel sends an email to Gov. Snyder's staff for a briefing memo which downplays health risks: "It's not like an imminent threat to public health."

February 10: The city of Flint retains an independent consulting firm, Veolia, to provide additional review and recommendations regarding the developing situation. Later, the state attorney general will file suit against Veolia.

February 16: The city of Flint posts its second FAQ that states the water is safe to drink.

February 18: The EPA, not MDEQ-ODWMA, collects a water sample at LeeAnn Walters' (a private citizen) residence. Walters had complained to city council and directly to the EPA.

February 25: Flint DPW's Glasgow also samples water in Walters' home and finds high lead levels—104 PPB, well above the 15 PPB required by SWDA. She (Walters) contacts the Chicago EPA.

February 26: The first internal EPA emails regarding the February 18 sampling results circulate: "WOW!!! Did he find LEAD! 104 parts per billion."

February 26: MDEQ's Busch emails colleagues: "As indicated by … [the first monitoring results] … the city is meeting 90th percentile. Not sure why region 5 (EPA) sees this one sample as such a big deal."

   Analysis: *Busch is a district supervisor at MDEQ who will later be criminally charged. This email once again indicates that MDEQ's "goal" was to meet the letter of the regulation and not to assure the public was supplied safe drinking water.*

February 27: The EPA's Miguel Del Toral voices concern that the Flint sampling method biases results to the low side. MDEQ's Bush responds that Walters' house is not part of the city's "established sample site pool," and that her residence has PVC plumbing.

March 3: Jerry Ambrose, the new Flint EM, tells the state that going back to DWSD water would increase the city's costs by $12 million.

March 12: Veolia issues its report to the city, which states that the water meets state and federal standards on TTHM control but does not mention lead. It also recommends corrosion control to address iron leaching from pipes. Estimated cost of the changes: $50,000.

March 13: MDEQ's Busch emails the Genessee County Health Department about the Legionellosis investigation. It implies that DEQ has no responsibilities because Legionella isn't regulated by the SWDA, and reminds GCHD that epidemiological investigation is GCHD's job, directing them to the Michigan Department of Health and Human Services (MDHHS).

April 25: The EPA's Del Toral emails MDEQ regarding concerns about the lack of corrosion control, pre-flushing and high lead levels. His memo says that the city of Flint does not appear to meet requirements for OCCT without treatment.

> **Analysis:** *This is the first time MDEQ is confronted on whether the SWDA has been violated.*

April 26: Del Toral emails EPA district 5 supervisor Tom Poy, and others, confirming that Flint has no corrosion control, which is "very concerning given the likelihood of lead service lines in city."

> **Analysis:** *EPA management is now clearly aware that there is a potential lead problem in Flint.*

April 27: MDEQ employees Cook, Busch, and Prysby exchange a series of emails about Del Toral's questions on corrosion control treatment (CCT).

Busch: "If he continues to persist, we may need Liane (Shekter-Smith) or director Wyant to make a call to EPA to help his over-reaches."

Cook: "I agree, the constant second guessing of how we interpret and implement our rules is getting tiresome."

April 29: Water samples taken from Walters' residence are sent to Virginia Tech. The average lead level is 2,429 PPB. The high was 13,200 PPB. Even after 25 minutes of flushing, the level was never below 200 PPB.

Analysis: *Keep in mind that the EPA limit is 15 PPB.*

May 1: Cook responds to Del Toral, indicating that MDEQ is delaying any decision pending completion of the second six-month monitoring period in June 2015. He says that since Flint will be switching water sources in another year, "requiring a (corrosion control treatment) study at the current time will be of little to no value."

Analysis: *It has been 13 months since the switch to Flint River water.*

June 25: MDEQ's Rosenthal emails Flint DPW employees Glasgow and Wright, reminding them that 61 more lead and copper samples need to be collected, "and that they will be [sic] below action level" (AL). As of now, with 39 results, the 90th percentile level is over the AL for lead.

Analysis: *This appears to suggest that the sampling should be done in a manner to get the "right" result. Later, as a result, Rosenthal is indicted on July 28, 2016.*

July 13:   MDEQ's Wurfel assures Michigan radio listeners that "anyone who is concerned about lead in the drinking water in Flint can relax … it does not look like there is any broad problem with the water supply freeing up lead as it goes into homes."

July 21: The EPA informs the MDEQ of its interpretation of SWDA-LCR and wants corrosion control implemented in Flint. The MDEQ responds to EPA via email saying it is premature and requests that the EPA concur with its approach.

July 23: The MDHHS emails a member of Gov. Snyder's staff saying the EPA employee Del Toral, who raised lead concerns, acted "outside of his authority."

July 27: The city of Flint provides MDEQ its original LCR report documenting lead levels sampling from January 1, 2015, to June 30, 2015. The report is later "scrubbed" after Flint meets with the MDEQ. The report is released on August 20 with the two high-lead results excluded.

August 4: At a meeting with residents, Shekter-Smith, the MDEQ-ODWMA supervisor, tells residents the whistleblower "Mr. Del Toral has been handled," and Flint residents will not be seeing him again.

August 17: The MDEQ tells Flint that based on the January to June 2015 monitoring results that CCT will have to be implemented. It recommends starting immediately, but gives the city six months to comply.

August 27: In a response to Gov. Snyder's staff inquiry about the high lead level in Walters' home, MDEQ's Wurfel replies: "This person is the one who had an EPA lead specialist come to her home and do tests, then released an unvetted draft of his report (that the EPA apologized to us profusely for) to the resident, who shared it with the ACLU, who promptly used it to continue raising hell with the locals … it's been rough sledding with a steady parade of community groups keeping everyone hopped-up and misinformed."

September 2: Virginia Tech reports elevated lead levels in Flint water, communicating that the corrosiveness of Flint water is causing lead to leach into residents' water. Its report reads, in part: "… the current Flint River water leaches **12X more lead to the water than Detroit water.**"

September 2: In response to the Virginia Tech report, Wurfel issues a press release stating: "We want to be very clear that the lead levels being detected in Flint drinking water are not coming from the treatment plant or the city's transmission lines. … The issue is how, or whether, and to what extent the drinking water is interacting with lead plumbing in people's home."

September 8: Virginia Tech emails Flint Mayor Dayne Walling: "I have no idea what MDEQ's agenda is, but based on their press releases and their actions to date, protecting the public and following federal laws does not seem to be a priority."

September 9: Wurfel tells Michigan media that "(VT) only

just arrived in town and (have) quickly proven the theory they set out to prove … offering broad, dire public health advice based on some quick testing could be seen as fanning political flames irresponsibly."

September 11: The MDEQ tells Michigan media that Flint is planning to have CCT in place by January 2016.

Analysis: Making it *18 months after the Flint River water (with no CCT) started flowing!*

September 15: Michigan media reports on Virginia Tech's statement that Flint's lead tests cannot be trusted due to flawed testing procedures: "Flint is the only city in America that I'm aware of that does not have a corrosion-control plan in place to stop this problem."

Wurfel responds: "The problem isn't new. It's just news now and a knee-jerk reaction would be an irresponsible response."

September 23: Flint Mayor Walling indicates he will issue an advisory and promote ways to minimize resident's exposure to lead. He tells doctors who have found high lead levels in children "that a return to purchasing water from Detroit would bankrupt the city."

September 25-26: Gov. Snyder's chief of staff emails the governor: "I can't figure out why the state is responsible, except that Dillon (state treasurer) did make the ultimate decision, so we're not able to avoid the subject. The real responsibility rests with the county, city, and KWA, but since the issue is the health of citizens and their children we're taking a proactive approach putting MDHHS out there as a communicator."

He adds: "Now we have the anti-everything group turning to the lead content. We can't tolerate the increased lead levels in any event, but it's really the city's water system that needs to deal with it."

September 29: Wurfel tells National Public Radio (NPR) that Del Toral's draft report is the work of a "rogue" employee.

October 2: As part of a press conference, there is a press release that says the water leaving the Flint water system is safe to drink but families with lead plumbing in their homes could have higher lead levels.

October 16: The DWSD and city of Flint execute a water supply contract and the city of Flint is reconnected to DWSD system.

Analysis: *The drinking water, which had not been treated for corrosion, had been flowing to the residents of Flint for 19 months!*

Before we go on, I have to share one more thing I found in a *Detroit Free Press* column by Nancy Kaffer, dated October 22, 2015. It contains the following email from Wurfel to state of Michigan Chief Treasurer Tom Saxton, Gov. Snyder's Chief of State Dennis Muchmore and MDEQ's Wyant:

Guys, here's an update and some clarification on the lead situation in Flint. Please limit this information to internal for now.

By the tenants of the federal statute, the city is in compliance for lead and copper. That aside, they have not optimized their water treatment (for the most part, this means adding phosphates to minimize the degree that water Ph mobilizes lead and copper in people' home plumbing).

Compliance with the standard started with testing. A June to December run of tests (all in homes with lead in their premise plumbing) concluded in December. Another January to June round of sampling concluded last month. Everything checks out in terms of compliance, but now the next step is optimizing the water supply.

So, in about two weeks, DEQ will be sending a formal communication about the optimizing issue. The federal program has long timelines for action. A community water supplier gets 18 months to study the options, and two years thereafter to implement water system implementation measures.

My Point: Conceivably, by the time we're halfway through the first timeline, the city will begin using a new water source with KWA ... and conceivably, the whole process starts all over again.

In terms of near-future issues, the bottom line is that residents of Flint do not need to worry about lead in their water supply, and DEQ's recent sampling does not indicate an imminent health threat from lead or copper. That said, anyone with lead pipes in their premise plumbing (this translates to tens of thousands of homes in our older centers, btw) should at least be aware they have them, and to some limited degree that's going to impart minute parts per billion of lead in the water no matter what. It's why nobody uses lead pipes anymore.

The column ends with this assessment by Kaffer:

I'm reminded of the old cliché: For evil to flourish, all that's required is that good people do nothing. In Flint, what happened was more insidious: For evil to flourish, all that is required is for people to do exactly, and only, what is required of them. Nothing less. Nothing more.

I must admit, my reaction to reading all of this was one of disbelief and outrage. I trust you had a similar reaction. However, as distasteful as this entire situation is—and continues to be to this day—it's worth revisiting it through the lens of the 10 questions I put forth and attempting to relate them to the six factors and six principles.

Let's start with organizational structure and its effect on lines of responsibility. The federal EPA has responsibility for safety of the water supply but delegated the responsibility for enforcement of the SWDA to the state of Michigan.

Did that absolve them of any responsibility for the water's safety? One might say it did, but at the very least, it had a responsibility to oversee that the state interpreted and enforced the law properly. The state of Michigan and the governor were given the EPA's responsibility to both see that the water was safe and that the requirements of the SWDA were met. The governor, in turn, delegated that responsibility to the MDEQ, who then assigned it to the ODWMA.

In a lot of ways, this made sense as there was no expertise in the governor's office for running a water system or enforcing the SWDA. In effect, this made the MDEQ-ODWMA the sole judge of what was required to meet the SWDA and deliver safe water. They, in turn, decided what the law required and what the system was required to do. They oversaw the Flint water system, but nobody was overseeing them.

Unfortunately, this made the decision-making process vulnerable to faults within the MDEQ and ODWMA organizations which, in my view, were many and deep. This was the fatal flaw that initiated the event.

However, the effects of organizational complexity did not stop there. The city of Flint and its utility department and water treatment plant are the actual water suppliers. In essence, the Flint WTP is the equivalent of GE, BP, or GM of the previous events—thus, the product supplier is clearly responsible for product safety. The product supplier generally is the best resource to understand the technology of its product and therefore has the best perspective on what the consequences of decisions are. In layman's terms, they "know what they are doing." In fact, Flint WTP's Glasgow directly questioned the MDEQ-ODWMA about corrosion treatment (note the timeline item dated April 16 and 17, 2014). But, if he questioned the plan, he had no recourse other than to go to the emergency manager, who was a state employee that reported to the state treasurer, who would depend on the MDEQ-ODWMA, a state agency, for advice.

Glasgow did not go to them. In later testimony, he

said he "felt at the time he didn't have the authority to make changes." In effect, he was following orders.

This organizational structure effectively separated the product supplier (the people with the best knowledge of the process) from the decision not to treat and also cut off its ability to appeal the decision.

One more observation on how organizational complexity blurs the lines of responsibility is evident in the timeline items from September 25 and 26, 2015. Even the governor's staff refused to recognize that the state (the "logo") was the party that was ultimately responsible. Without a doubt, this convoluted government organizational structure blurred the lines of responsibility enough that it allowed a (now I get to use the term) "rogue agency" to make a decision that would impact the lives of the citizens of Flint for a long, long time.

Now, let's focus on money and how it played a clear role in influencing many of the decisions that were made.

In this entire tragedy, politics empowered the "money elephant" to the point where almost nothing else could be heard. The governor ran on a plank of tough fiscal restraint and made it clear that fiscal considerations were at the top of his "goals" list. Look no further than appointing an EM that reported to the state treasurer to see what his priorities were. When anyone inside the state government looked around they knew what the number one goal was: save money.

Despite this, I remain troubled trying to understand how the "money elephant" influenced the people in the MDEQ/ODWMA. Even after deep analysis of the situation, I cannot find any direct connection between the "save money" goal and the agency's measurements. Of course, they were aware of the money issue, but it seems unlikely that they would have risked the safety of the water to save the city a relatively small amount of money.

This leaves only one other thought: They did not even think about the value product safety at all. In their minds, the value elephant wasn't just silent, it was non-existent. Under this scenario, I would surmise they thought their only responsibility was to meet the literal requirements of the SWDA /LCR. Thus, I do not believe they ever thought about the residents of Flint and their basic need to have safe drinking water. They perceived no risk. The only risk they perceived was whether the law's requirements were met.

This is where bureaucracy comes into play. The dictionary defines bureaucracy as "a system of government by groups of officials each dealing with its own kind of business …" The MDEQ/ODWMA's kind of business was limited to paper, not water. This type of bureaucratic thinking must also have permeated the organization's culture and distorted it in a way that drove them to behave in, what I can only describe as a bizarre fashion. The decision to not treat for lead was clearly irrational and irresponsible as it was known that as the water flowed the pipes would corrode. Their combined defiance and disregard for the evidence the water was tainted was arrogant and dismissive. Their manipulation of the monitoring results, lingering defense of their actions and their deceit of the public, Virginia Tech, and even the EPA was unconscionable at best and immoral at worst. There are no kind words to describe the culture, nor the motives for that organization. I will say, however, that as of this writing, five members of the MDEQ have been criminally indicted by the Michigan attorney general. As pointed out previously, culture matters. It really does.

Before we go on, there is one more assault the MDEQ made on anyone's sense of right or wrong: its assertion that the citizens of Flint were responsible for the lead in the water because they had lead pipes.

This is referred to in the timeline item dated October 2, 2015, where internal discussions among themselves led them to conclude that water leaving the Flint water system was safe to drink, but families with lead plumbing in their homes could have higher lead levels. The MDEQ even had the audacity to use that answer in their testimony to Congress when they were eventually questioned about their actions.

There were several other agencies that were deeply involved in this doomsday event. The Michigan Department of Health and Human Services (MDHHS) was cited by the Michigan attorney general as being a key player in denying there was a problem and misinforming the public. As of this writing, three MDHHS employees have been criminally indicted, along with the five from the MDEQ.

Finally, it's worth mentioning the way the EPA's Del Toral was treated after he brought up his concerns for what was going on in Flint. As a whistleblower, he was instrumental in identifying that there was a real lead problem, that the requirements of the SWDA were not being met, and that the monitoring techniques being used by the Flint parties were incorrect. Del Toral's actions were met with attacks from the MDEQ, the MDHHS, and even inside the EPA.

In an email sent from a personal account, Michigan EPA program manager, Jennifer Crooks, instructed Michigan environmental regulators on how to "truthfully" tell "the legislature or whoever" that they had never officially received Del Toral's report.

He was called a "rogue employee" by the MDEQ in

an NPR report, and the MDEQ contemplated calling his management to complain about his overreaches and second guessing. They even told residents that "he had been handled and they will not see him again."

Virginia Tech professor Marc Edwards, the independent researcher who helped prove the presence of high lead levels, commented: "Standard retaliation for heroic actors in government science agencies is to watch as your legitimate concerns are ignored, ethical actions are termed 'inappropriate,' harm to the public continues unabated, friends stand silent in acquiescence to the shunning, and your reputation is publicly discredited." He further noted: "Mr. Del Toral was given the full treatment."

How employees can bring up concerns and have them appropriately addressed is critical. It's one of the most important points of this book and something we'll tackle later.

Let's close out the Flint water crisis event by considering that there are several points that need to be made on consequences to the organization that is ultimately responsible (the "logo") and consequences to the individual employees that were involved.

As I read through everything I could find on Flint, I kept trying to identify what organization would be ultimately responsible and suffer the consequences. In this case, I believe all the organizations were responsible because none of them were responsible. To be just, they all should suffer consequences. In fact, they all did because the consequences for them were a complete loss of the public's trust. But since this is government, there were no financial consequences (except for the residents and taxpayers).

On the other hand, there were no business

consequences. Today, it is business as usual. When politics and bureaucracy mix with making decisions, strange things can happen.

But what about the individual employees?

In the Flint case, there have been a number of jobs lost and a still-growing number of criminal indictments. That might always be the case where it is determined that laws have been broken. But that is not the only consequence for the people involved. There can be psychological effects that last for a lifetime. This is especially true for events which lead to loss of life. I know that the UA 232 event affected me deeply. Therefore, I must admit I am wondering if those involved with the Flint event will have the same experience. Only God will know.

The scorecard:

Decision Factors that Apply 3+ of 6

Of the six influence factors, clearly values, culture, and organizational complexity stand out as being the most prominent.

But it is a sad thing to say that this series of events and decisions is so incomprehensible that I don't understand the roles that goals, measurements or perception of risk played. Certainly, the state's goal of saving money was clear, but the MDEQ had no financial measurements. Their value should have been product safety but instead it seemed to be meeting the letter but not the intent of the Safe Water Drinking Act. That led to a perception that unsafe water was not the threat.

In other words, they had no perception of the real risk. Incredible!

Principles Violated 5+ of 6

Relative to the principles, all apply with possibly one exception: The governor certainly did not communicate the values of product safety and ethical behavior. The culture was one which was directed at protecting the reputation of the state agencies. The "do not treat" decision was made inside state agencies and disregarded outside opinions. Trust but verify would have applied both to the EPA and the state of Michigan. The EPA delegated their responsibility to enforce the SWDA to the state but did not follow up to see that is was done. The state did not follow up to see that its own agencies were in fact focused on protecting the citizens. And, last but not least, is the fact that there was no well-defined process for employees inside the state or city organizations to bring up issues of concern to the state of Michigan.

That leaves the principle "the logo is responsible so the logo should make the decision." I would submit that in this case the logo is the state of Michigan and the logo did make the decision. Unfortunately, it made the decision while not adhering to any of the other five principles we have been talking about. The result was a tragedy!

Chapter 13
Self-Inflicted Wounds

In 1999, engineers in the Audi division of Volkswagen landed on a solution to reduce a pesky clattering noise that its 3.0-liter V6 diesel engine made while idling. The engineers' solution, however, became the root cause of yet another doomsday event. Like Flint, VW's problem was initiated by people inside its own organization. Unlike the BP oil spill, GM's ignition switch trouble, or even the United Airlines 232 disaster, there was no uncertainty about whether a doomsday event would ever occur.

VW's troubles were a toxic combination of strongly emphasized goals and a culture that rewarded success without asking how that success was achieved. While perception of risk and measurements also played a role, organizational complexity did not. Further, the VW diesel emissions scandal did not involve product safety. Instead, it was the case of someone who got away with doing something wrong in the past thinking they could do it again without getting caught. In a word: cheating.

To achieve their miracle solution to the clattering noise, VW engineers determined they could inject additional fuel into the engine upon ignition. Unfortunately, this significantly increased emissions, which was a non-starter because of emissions regulations. So, to solve this problem, the engineers developed what they called the "acoustic function"—software which sensed when the engine was being tested for emissions and turned off the added fuel. This made the engine clatter again, but it lowered the emissions so that the vehicle would once again meet requirements. Satisfied with the solution, VW's acoustic function was used on European market 3.0-liter diesel V6 Audis from 2004 to 2008.

In the years since, VW has been accused of using the term "acoustic function" as a code phrase to mask the software's true purpose.

In 2005, VW announced a campaign designed to sell more diesel-powered cars in the U.S., centered on the smaller 2.0-liter TDI engine. By this time, the U.S. emissions requirements had become more stringent than in Europe. The VW engineers found themselves stuck between a rock and a hard place because they knew the U.S. emissions regulations would be very difficult to meet—in fact, they described them as "impossible." That's because when the EPA conducts emissions tests, the manufacturer must disclose the use of any "auxiliary emissions control devices" which change the car's emissions as a function of situational factors. Devices that affect the effectiveness of emissions controls outside of testing parameters are called "defeat devices," and are considered cheating the system.

As a result, the VW engineers considered three options to solve their problem:

1. Use selective catalytic reduction (SCR), which was complex, costly, and required licensing from Mercedes. This option was considered distasteful to VW, which billed itself as a "proud" engineering organization.
2. Utilize a lean trap system, which had the unacceptable side effect of clogging the engine's soot filter.
3. Resort to the "acoustic function" (by definition

a defeat device), which was pioneered on the Audi several years before. Engineers knew if they did not disclose the device's use, the engine would meet U.S. emissions requirements and the system would be both less complex and cheaper to produce.

Option No. 3 was just too good to pass up.

As time progressed, however, the International Council of Clean Transportation noticed a discrepancy between the emissions levels reported to European and U.S. regulators. The ICCT then funded West Virginia University to conduct testing to determine why.

WVU researchers devised a test which measured emissions while the car was actually being driven on the road as opposed to the laboratory conditions which activated the defeat device. The results reported were eye-popping—up to 40 times worse depending on how the car was being driven. This was in early 2014. Between then and August 2015, VW denied the use of a defeat device, claiming instead the discrepancies were mere technical glitches. Finally, when confronted with the evidence and a threat from regulators that they would not approve the sale of 2016 models, VW admitted using the defeat device.

As of this writing, the consequences for VW's decision remain "undefined." They do, however, include the following so far:

- Removal of the company's CEO.
- Massive recalls and buybacks of cars.
- Stoppage of new car sales of some models, including Audis and Porsches.
- Increased oversight of VW products

by regulatory agencies worldwide.

- Lawsuits by the U.S. Department of Justice and several states' attorney generals.
- A massive loss of reputation and confidence in the VW brand
- Financial liabilities in excess of $18 billion.
- Potential criminal prosecution of individuals inside the organization including top management.

From an organizational standpoint, and for the people involved, this scandal meets the definition of a doomsday event because of the scope and the consequences. But it did not have to happen. VW and its engineers brought it on themselves.

The real reasons why this happened may never actually be known, but there are several inferred reasons that potentially led to the issue. First, and most critical, was VW's inherent culture. As a nearly 80-year-old institution, VW has had a long history of success. Depending on which benchmark you use, VW is either the first or second leading automobile manufacturer in the world. Its brands are iconic and include Audi, Porsche and Lamborghini. The *New York Times* described VW's culture as "confident, cutthroat, and insular."

That adjective "insular" rings alarm bells when it comes to respecting the interests of those outside the organization—regulators and governments included.

Former VW CEO Martin Winterkorn, who resigned in the wake of the scandal, was known as a demanding manager who abhorred failure. Reuters described his management style as "fostering a climate of fear, an authoritarianism that went unchecked." As the son of a German immigrant, I understand this management style better than most people. It creates a situation where you are expected to do as you are told and where failure is not well accepted. Another thing not well accepted is complaining about how difficult a task may be to accomplish. In the minds of these types of people, there's just one goal: Get the job done.

Understanding this, I'm sure that after the engineers analyzed the three options, they were painfully aware of what they needed to do. Sadly, this became more evident after a 2016 statement released by VW said:

"A group of powertrain employees decided that by changing 'only a small number of an approximately 15,000 individual algorithms' in the engine management software, the diesel engines could meet the emissions targets' within the budget that was available for the development of the engine management software and without the need to involve superior levels …"

This speaks clearly about the style of management these men worked under, and its effect on the willingness or unwillingness of those inside the organization to bring up issues that could derail the company's goals and long-term plans. It also reveals how aware the engineers were about their cost measurements.

And what of the perception of risk that so often gets ignored and leads to doomsday events?

There were three things which distorted both the engineers' and company's perception of risk. First, they simply had no idea of how catastrophic the consequences of an event that was attributed to unethical behavior could be for the company. In fact, I don't think anyone did. Second, the defeat device was used before and nothing negative happened to VW—or the people who owned and drove the cars. Finally, the cheating was accomplished with only software. Who would actually know what was happening? As VW itself reported: "It was only a small number of approximately 15,000 individual algorithms …"

And the scorecard:

Decision Factors that Apply 5 of 6

Five of the six influence factors came into play leading up to this event. Clearly values, culture and goals were the most prominent. However, the perception of risk was also influential for two reasons. First, they had used the defeat device before and did not get caught. Second, they didn't expect a few lines of code would be detected. That brings in the factor of measurements. Using the defeat device helped them meet the measurement of fixing the problem using the lowest cost solution.

Principles Violated 2+ of 6

Of the six principles, certainly the two regarding values and culture are the most applicable. VW's CEO made it clear what the goal was—sell diesel-powered cars in the US. And he sent that message into an organizational culture that was defined as being responsive to its leadership. The result was fully predictable. Did the logo make the decision? Certainly, it was made at least at the middle level of the organization. I will leave it to others to determine if it was made at a higher level. However, if it was, the VW leadership failed in their responsibility to protect their organization from the doomsday event. The principle regarding the logo making the decision can't protect any organization from that!

Let's close the VW doomsday event with a quote from a VW advisory board member musing about the issue: "We need in (the) future a climate in which problems are not hidden but can be openly communicated to superiors … We need a culture in which it is possible to argue with your superior about the best way to go."

Chapter 14
Leadership

After taking you through the VW and Flint events, I would be remiss if I didn't say a few more words about the responsibility and influence that upper level management has when it comes to either causing or avoiding doomsday events.

Clearly, those at the top of the organization will be held accountable should a doomsday event occur. The "excuse" that they didn't know about the issue or did not participate in the decision-making process will simply not be accepted by the outside world. They are at the head of the organization and they had the responsibility to communicate the values and set the culture for the entire organization.

At BP, the money elephant and the schedule measurement were obviously the driving force behind the decisions made. At VW, the message "sell diesels in the U.S." was clear. In Michigan, the governor was elected on a "save money" platform, and the emergency managers of Flint reported to the state treasurer. There should be no doubt about who sent those messages. Even in the GM event, the revolving door at the top of the organization influenced how the ignition switch problem was handled.

Whether they realize it or not, the words and particularly the actions of those at the very top of the organization have a great influence on how and what people do when they are faced with difficult decisions. The words "body language" immediately come to mind. Earlier I described organizational culture as "a feeling which is developed throughout time while working with or inside an organization" and that "culture is the way individuals judge what their surrounding world considers acceptable behavior." I know that as I went through my career, I would pay careful attention to what the upper levels of the organization talked about and what decisions they made when faced with the "money vs. value" dilemma. Did money win or did safety win? Did they hide an issue or did they report it and make the customer whole? That is the way I got the "feeling" for how the organization did its business.

This is what leadership is all about: Those at the top are always on a stage and their actions and words are being used to mold the very culture of the enterprise. And, as I said before, culture matters—it really matters.

Chapter 15
The "Three Worlds"

The six principles laid out in the previous chapters describe what an organization needs to do to avoid experiencing a doomsday event. The challenge, however, is adhering to these principles. Before we get to that, it is important to look at what a corporation is and how humans and corporations interact. I like to think of this as the confluence of "three worlds."

The dictionary defines an organization as "a group of persons united for some purpose." They are also defined as "a group of persons who obtain a charter giving them certain legal rights and privileges. A corporation can buy, sell, and own property, manufacture and ship products, and bring lawsuits as if its members were a single person."

Organizations or corporations themselves are inanimate but, in fact, they are made up of human beings who think and make decisions for them. In effect, humans are the brains of the corporation. And since humans think for the corporation, much like the human family, the corporation has its own values and culture. I'll call this the "corporate world."

Humans inside the organization, however, not only think for the organization or corporation, but they also think for themselves as individuals. As a result, they are subject to every influence that makes up their own value system, culture, and personality. I'll call this the "personal world."

That leaves the "outside world." The outside world is anybody outside the corporation. Governments, customers, regulators, the legal system, and any other body that is in a position to bring consequences to the logo in case of a doomsday event. The outside world is, therefore, the ultimate judge and jury. This is precisely the reason for the principle, "The logo is responsible, so the logo should make the decision." Unfortunately, doing that is difficult because any decision made by the logo depends on how the corporate and personal worlds interact.

Employees live in two worlds—the personal world and the corporate world. Sometimes that makes it difficult to get people to act with the interests of the enterprise valued above their own. They are asked to put themselves into the corporate world even if that means there is an impact on them as a member of their own personal world. For example, if you are measured on delivering a product on time, you might be reluctant to delay that delivery even though you see a potential problem. Raising that problem might impact how your boss evaluates your work. Simply put, it is hard to ignore the things you are being measured on in the interest of avoiding an event that may never happen. This is where the principles regarding values and culture come into play. Without them, people would almost certainly choose the direction which benefits their personal world over that of the corporate world.

The corporate world is certainly not immune to near-term parochial pressures either. No organization or corporation will remain in business very long if it doesn't meet its self-proclaimed measurements. Did we ship the product? Did we make the quarterly numbers? All of these bring the same tension to the corporate world that is experienced in the personal world. Can we meet near-term goals and measurements and still avoid causing a major event? It was precisely this type of decision that people at BP were faced with when they were capping the well. Having faced a similar dilemma, myself, I can attest that these decisions are difficult ones to make.

Hopefully adhering to the six principles makes solving that dilemma easier. That leads back to the question posed above: How can that be done?

I'll use the approach we took at GE Aircraft Engines to work potential product safety issues as an example of how to do it. Before I do, it is important to note that whatever the approach, it must be tailored to reflect the way each organization does its business.

First, let me explain how we at GE Aircraft Engines were organized and then how we institutionalized the process to make decisions about product safety related issues. In the next chapter, I'll explore how those processes work. I'll also share a few of the issues that cropped up as we tried to implement the process.

The organizational approach we chose was aimed at adhering to the two principles: the logo should make the decision and base decisions on diverse input. We used a two-tier approach.

Tier one was set up in the organization that owned the product—the working level. Tier two was stationed at the vice president level—the logo level.

The GE Aircraft Engines organization, like many large businesses, is complex so I will only use one department as an example. The CF6 Project Department had responsibility for the family of engines which powered airplanes like the 747 and A330. When I say responsibility, I mean total responsibility—including everything from the configuration of the engines to funding development programs, schedules for shipping, customer interface, and even marketing plans. The rest of the organization—supply chain, engineering, etc.—supported their efforts. This organization was also the one with control of the money. They were fully responsible for the product and for meeting the programs' measurements. Everyone understood who was responsible for the CF6 product line. Effectively, their role was to be the owner of the CF6 family of engines. They were responsible for getting the engines built, delivering them to the customers, and assuring that the customers were happy with their products. They also had the responsibility to assure the safety of their product line. This was done by forming what we called a Safety Program Management Team (SPMT) within the CF6 Project which was led by a manager who also had control of the configuration of the product.

This organizational approach was institutionalized by a formal company policy that covered the product safety process. It outlined how issues could be brought up to the CF6 SPMT and clearly defined what the team was responsible to do. This included such things as maintaining a worklist, assuring timely follow up, evaluating safety concerns, ensuring root cause analysis is completed, etc. The SPMT was the place where issues got raised, decisions got made as to their criticality, and follow-up action plans were developed. They were also responsible to see that those plans were funded and executed.

But what about the dilemma we talked about earlier? Wouldn't the CF6 Project be subject to the pressures of meeting the near-term measurements? Isn't that putting the fox in the henhouse?

The answer is yes and no.

Of course, a product-oriented organization would be

concerned about their near-term measurements. However, that organization is the one with the resources and the power to get things done. It simply is a reality that the power and the responsibility to act should be in the hands of the organization with the money. That is why I call it the working level.

The other reason to put it there is to be sure the organization maintains ownership for the product. This, along with a diverse makeup of the SPMT, in my view, made the CF6 Project the right place to raise potential safety issues on CF6 engines. They knew the product; they knew the customers; and they had the ability to formulate effective programs that would address issues while best managing the impact on the daily workings of the business.

However, the SPMT was only the first tier. In recognition of the principle regarding the logo making the decision, the company policy also put a second tier in place which was made up at the logo level. This was done by forming what was called a Product Safety Review Board (PSRB) comprised of all the vice presidents of the business. The intent was to assure that the interests of the enterprise were being considered over the more parochial interests of the individual programs. This also brought another benefit by involving people with a wider range of perspectives to the decision-making process. The PSRB represented the logo, brought a diverse perspective, and served as a check and balance for the decisions of the PSRB—trust, but verify.

Note that by having a formal policy, everyone at all levels knew what they were responsible for and how the decision process was to be done. This also brought structure and discipline to the process.

We used the above two-tiered approach at GE Aircraft Engines. It proved to be effective and is still in place today. However, every organization has its own characteristics and it is important to tailor the decision process to fit its needs.

An example of when a three-tiered architecture might be appropriate is when the upper levels of management do not have the expertise or the time to become involved in the details of an issue. In that case, the second tier could be an advisory board analogous to the classic board of directors. This de facto advisory board could be comprised of independent and diverse thinkers who have no direct daily responsibilities within that business. They would be there to strictly protect the logo and give their opinion on how the outside world might view the decisions and actions of the logo should an event occur.

This approach could easily be applied to either product safety or ethical issues. Such an advisory board would report to the logo level to advise them about decisions and programs put forth by the working level. This "advisory board" could take the time to ask the right questions and get a better general perspective on a given issue. The board could then make recommendations to the logo level for their review and decision. Such an approach reinforces the diverse thinking principle while still allowing the logo to determine its own fate.

Clearly, whatever the approach, the importance of independent and diverse thought while having the logo make the final decisions is at the heart of meeting the intent of the six principles. If nothing else, if a doomsday event occurs, the organization can look back and say, "It was the best we could have done." Without these principles in place, I guarantee that, should an event occur, the consequences which befall the logo will be far greater.

Like anything else, putting the theory into practice presents numerous practical problems. Some are what I might call philosophical questions and others are more closely related to how humans react when their judgment is questioned. I'll discuss some of these implementation issues in the next chapters.

Before we go on, there is one last point that needs to be made regarding the "personal world." It is the understanding that we, as humans, possess some things that organizations and corporations do not—emotions, memories, and hopefully, a personal sense of responsibility. While organizations do not sustain psychological consequences as a result of their actions, humans do.

Chapter 16
Raising Issues

"The logo is responsible so the logo should make the decision."

If the "logo" doesn't know about issues, it obviously can't address them. Therefore, the first and probably the most important step is to bring potential issues to the attention of the organization. Usually, when big, complex organizations are engaged in big, complex projects, there are many things that have the potential for causing serious problems.

Every day, people are getting paid to solve problems in their area of expertise. But when should they raise issues to the logo? There are similar questions when there are field events which do not have serious consequences. They weren't serious at the time but will they be the next? The reality here is that there are no easy answers.

Consider the UA 232 event at Sioux City, Iowa. Those familiar with the titanium melting process knew that the process had the potential for producing defects. The people who were familiar with the inspection processes knew that they had vulnerabilities. I, and the product support manager, debated whether to add an inspection for fan discs. We all made decisions on our own to do what we did. We reacted to the values, the culture, and the perception of risk that each of us had. We accepted that what we were doing was in accordance with the "way things were done at the time." After all, there were four "precursor" (field) events with no fatalities.

In her book, "The Challenger Launch Decision", Diane Vaughn *(University of Chicago Press, 1996)* coined the phrase, "the normalization of deviance." It refers to when defects are accepted because they have occurred before and have not resulted in unacceptable consequences. Before the Challenger disaster, shuttles experienced o-ring burning events, but none of them resulted in failure. Then, on a colder day, the results were tragic! Normalizing deviance is one of the most common reasons for lowering the perception of risk. It adheres to the old adage, "It was OK before, so it will be OK again." Unfortunately, the past is not a predictor of the future.

Even folks at BP who decided to cap the well against the advice of Halliburton claimed they had done it that way before and nothing bad had happened. In the VW case, they cheated at least once before—on the Audi—and used software to change results. But they weren't caught before. In case after case, the logo was unaware of the threat and did not have the opportunity to weigh in on the acceptable course of action. This reinforces the need to raise issues to the logo level because it puts the responsibility for the decision where it belongs and brings diversity of perspective into making decisions. It also puts the problem at the level of the organization, which has the resources to take whatever action is required.

There are three other principles vital for getting issues raised from inside an organization—values, culture, and having a defined process.

An enterprise's values must be constantly reinforced by management if they are to be considered when an employee faces the "should I raise this issue?" decision. It's imperative that the values they respond to represent doing what's in the outside world's and the corporate world's best interests.

Having the "right" culture means the organization is

committed to nurturing a feeling that management wants to hear about issues. Everyone should feel like they can raise issues and get help in deciding what needs to be done. In big, complex organizations, this can be hard to accomplish. Think about it: When you were a child, you didn't want to go to your parents and tell them about something bad, did you? It took guts and a sense that your parents wanted to hear the bad as well as the good. It also meant you believed that they would help you with the problem.

Communicating in a family is different than communicating to the "big bosses" in an organization. There must be a defined way to do that. We did that at GE Aircraft Engines by creating the formal company policy that spelled out an employee's responsibility to bring up issues and how to do it. That became part of our culture.

Usually big projects involve supporting organizations like contractors or suppliers. It is also important that they, too, understand how to raise potential issues. Take for example Halliburton's knowledge that the well-capping procedure that BP intended to use was not, in their opinion, safe. Had Halliburton at the logo level told BP at the logo level about their concerns, it's possible the event would never have happened.

That said, it's more likely that nobody at the logo level within Halliburton even knew that some of their employees had concerns. But, assuming Halliburton did know, they would have had to make the decision to approach one of their biggest customers and tell them they were making a serious mistake. This additional nightmare scenario might have even meant a decision on their part to refuse to do the work as directed by BP! (Note the influence of measurements and goals.)

The way around this dilemma is for the prime contractor and the supplier to have a formal relationship mirroring the relationship explored earlier in this chapter, where the supplier feels responsible for bringing up issues and has a contractually defined way of doing that. Had BP and Halliburton had such a relationship, possibly neither Halliburton nor BP would have suffered the consequences. Conversely, had BP not taken Halliburton's advice, the worst consequence they would have suffered may have been only the loss of a customer—instead of loss of life and an environmental disaster.

Field events always have their own characteristics. Sometimes, the events are easy to interpret and the remediation plan is clear. Other times, things are much subtler—like the GM airbag non-deployment. Cases like this are far more difficult to manage as they confound and delay getting the correct action plan in place.

The bottom line to all of this is that the decision and planning process cannot work unless potential threats are brought into the system. That only happens if the right values and culture are in place and the system is institutionalized.

Obviously, encouraging issues to be raised will result in a significant number of issues that will need to be evaluated and decisions made as to how to react to them. The challenge therefore is to identify the things which truly have the potential to threaten the enterprise and to relegate the others to be worked as "normal course of business." No organization has enough resources to simultaneously tackle every issue with the intensity required to mitigate critical threats. If they try to do that, the risk is to fall into the "if everything is critical, nothing is critical" trap.

Chapter 17
Everything = Nothing

I know of no big, complicated, or technically advanced projects that don't involve risk or have no problems. Therefore, if doomsday events are to be avoided, it is critical to separate out the significant threats from the items which can be handled in the normal course of business. But how? Unfortunately, there isn't any simple answer! It is one of the single most difficult and most important decisions that the logo must make.

When I was the chief engineer at GE Aircraft Engines, one of my responsibilities was to manage the Flight Safety Office. That responsibility, coupled with my involvement in numerous design-related issues, brought me in contact with a variety of problems—any of which could potentially have serious consequences. At the same time, I found myself serving as a semi-counselor to team members as they would come into my office and ask me to help them decide whether a problem was being treated with the appropriate urgency. Fundamentally, I was being asked to judge whether an issue had the potential to lead up to a doomsday event. The implications of such decisions are great. If you are right, an event might be avoided. If you are wrong, an opportunity might be lost!

My office was on the second floor of a building which faced Interstate 75. I remember sitting there and looking out the window at cars passing by and reflecting on a problem that somebody brought to my attention. I kept wishing that God would come down and tell me what to do—He never did!

Every individual in the organization who knows of a problem faces the same dilemma when they try to decide to raise that issue with his or her boss. Sure, it can be scary. But in reality, it is the most important decision anyone can make. By deciding to go forward, an individual is, in effect, putting the difficult decision in the hands of the logo, where it belongs. This is exactly the right course of action because it brings diversity of thought, application of appropriate resources, and places responsibility with the logo.

Once issues are raised, however, the organization is faced with the same decision: is it a threat, or can it be worked in the normal course of business? Since the deity won't help, this decision is left up to the judgment and perspectives of the people who live in both the corporate and personal worlds and who are subject to the six factors which influence how people make decisions.

The reality here is that there is no magic formula. The best that can be done is to adhere to the principles, follow the process, and trust that the people involved will make a decision which balances the values of the enterprise with the pressures of running the business. No matter what the outcome, it is always a good thing when the logo is in a position to make critical decisions about how and when to react to a threat.

To close out this chapter, I thought I would take you through numerous roadblocks that we at GE faced when trying to implement our product safety process. They illustrate how difficult it is to make decisions like this, and how different people perceive risk and responsibility. Note that none of these questions have crisp, clear answers.

The first question was: What is safety? People wanted a definition. To me, the obvious answer was: It is safety if somebody is going to get hurt. I quickly ran into, what I call, the regulatory mindset. This can be described by the "what if" question. What if this? What if that? In other words, a mindset that continues to formulate "what if" questions until everything eventually becomes a safety issue. Unfortunately, this type of reasoning is a manifestation of the fact that everyone has a different perception of risk. Perception of risk is a significant factor in making any decisions that may carry significant consequences and it is the main reason for the principle regarding making decisions based on diverse input.

When faced with that "what if" question, the approach I took was to use simple examples as guidance. I would tell the person that an engine shutdown on a two- or four-engine airplane is not a safety issue. That's because pilots are trained to handle that situation and industry experience shows the situation can be managed safely.

Another example would be the failure of a turbine blade which causes an engine to shut down. There have been many turbine blade failures throughout the years. These are certainly operational problems, but they have not led to people getting hurt. These have been handled in a safe and well proven manner.

That doesn't mean that engine shutdowns are not a threat. Take the example of the shutdown being caused by an environmental threat, such as rain, ice, or birds. Any of these might lead to the shutdown of not just one engine but of all the engines. Needless to say, this situation is classified differently and merits the label "critical."

These "what is safety" and "what if" questions are representative of the inherent difficulties in making the critical versus non-critical judgments. If you are in a business where the general public are the users, you will be faced with any number of unusual events which, most likely, can be attributed to the user doing something that was not anticipated. Is it reasonable to expect the logo to respond to every one of these events? The answer depends on the perception of risk. Will it happen more often? If the assessment is "no," then a response is probably not warranted.

Let's go back a number of years to when a bottle of Tylenol was found to have been contaminated while on the shelf. Even in the worst-case scenario, you would not have expected that many people would have been harmed. However, the random possibility that I might be the person who was harmed would have kept me from buying Tylenol. Since many people would think the same way, it's not a stretch to believe they would have simply stopped buying the product rather than open themselves up to the possible danger of being poisoned. This made the problem a threat to the existence of the business, which meant it demanded a nuclear response. The decision to fully recall the product saved the company.

This illustrates the importance of having a decision-making process that evaluates events on a one-by-one basis and, for each of them, makes an objective "critical versus non-critical" decision.

Ethical events are a bit different. I believe the critical versus non-critical decision depends on whether the outside world would judge the issue to be a result of the logo's general business practices rather than the result of a single individual's actions. In the 2016 Wells Fargo scandal, where employees participated in a scheme to set up unauthorized accounts, it brought the business practices of the entire bank into question. Consumers began to ask themselves whether they wanted to deal with a bank that threw ethics into the wind. Needless to say, this issue had to be addressed as critical.

The next thing I ran into at GE was the desire to have a quantitative way to assess risk. Being an engineer, that means making a number. If you can calculate the probability of an event happening, that will give you a clear way of deciding if the event will ever happen. This is exactly what we were trying to do prior to the UA 232 event. We took all the data that we could find and made numerous attempts to predict how likely it would be to experience a failure. Since the available data was questionable and incomplete, we had little confidence in the results. However, that didn't stop us from trying to get more and better data. That search led us to not make any specific decisions at all! The ironic part of that story is that one of those predictions was very close to being right. But because we were spooked by the flawed data, we didn't believe that result, either.

I learned several things from this experience. First, the desire to have a methodology in place that helps you make any critical decision is strong. Second, the results of any probability analysis are heavily dependent on the input data. Getting good input data is very hard. Third, the past does not necessarily predict the future.

Despite all of this, however, I still believe that such predictions have a place in the decision-making process. They should just be one way of providing some guidance of what the risk level might be. If they are used like that and not taken as, "if the risk is below this number we are OK" or "if the risk is above this number, we need to do something," they become useful. Putting too much faith in these predictions can become troublesome as there are too many variables that are not considered which may drastically impact the outcome.

Once again, God will not come down and tell you what to do. Every potential issue must be reviewed and the decision determined based on the circumstances and consequences. Unfortunately, there are no cookbook answers. The best advice I can offer is to bring the best and most diverse mental resources at your disposal to the process. Even then, sometimes you will be right and sometimes you will be wrong. Even if you are wrong, then all can say with a clear conscience: We did the best that we could do with what we knew.

Chapter 18
Formulating a Plan

Once an issue is identified as having the potential to cause a doomsday event, it is time to decide what, how, and when to do something about it. Making these decisions is almost as difficult as the decision to move forward as they, too, depend heavily on the perception of risk.

Issues that are hardware-related are significantly more difficult to handle than issues that aren't. That's because there are significant technical issues to address before you can formulate a good plan: Is the root cause of the problem understood? Is a proven redesign available? Can enough replacement parts be made at a sufficient rate to lower the risk to the desired level? Does the redesign meet all regulatory requirements? How does the plan impact the direct customer? Will the user incorporate the fix?

Compounding those problems are business questions that arise as well: Are there resources available to accomplish implementation of the plan? What will the customer's reaction be? Will the plan increase or decrease our liability?

Another reason that deciding on a mitigation plan is difficult is that it must include timing. Often, the question becomes: How fast do we need to lower the risk to an acceptable level? Whatever the ultimate plan, its success will depend on how well it fits within the above constraints.

My experience at GE almost always involved issues that were uncovered by field events. That meant there were engines out in the fleet that could potentially have the same problem. Obviously, the longer the time it took to take action, the higher the probability of having another failure. This put the timing decision front and center.

Another reality we faced was that making changes to a jet engine is not easy. The root cause of the problem may not be easily understood; there may not be parts available; or a redesign may have to be done and certified. These scenarios take time, which in turn increases the risk of another failure. If you recall the GM ignition switch case, determining root cause significantly delayed getting the problem addressed.

One obvious solution in cases like this would be to stop everything and recall the product until a fix is identified and new product can be put into the field. I call that the nuclear option because it brings such dire consequences to both the organization and the customer base that it is usually not an option at all. There are times when the nuclear option is the only option. Recall the Tylenol incident, which occurred in the days before consumable items had sealed packaging. At first, nobody could figure out where the contamination was coming from or how widespread it was. In a landmark decision by James Burke, Tylenol's then-CEO, he pulled all the product from the shelves and asked that it be returned for a full refund. Obviously, this had a huge impact on the company's short-term measurements, but in the long run it essentially saved the company. It was a gutsy decision that was driven by the company's culture and Burke's perception of risk. He wanted to send a message to everyone that their wellbeing took priority over the company's goals and measurements. I'm convinced he was also thinking about the damage another event would have had on the company's reputation. He was right in both cases.

In the jet engine business, grounding the fleet means that airlines can't use their airplanes, their customers can't get to where they are going, and the reputation of the engine company is seriously damaged. That means there must be a way of managing the risks while finding the root cause of the problem, manufacturing the necessary product, and getting it into service. This is called a containment plan. The purpose of a containment plan is to lower risks to a level which is temporarily acceptable while providing time to develop and execute a long-term plan. Eliminating the hard alpha risk in titanium took almost a decade because the industry had to make fundamental changes to the melting process and install the infrastructure to do it.

There are many approaches which can be used to provide significant risk reduction while providing time for the full solution to be implemented. Is there a limited population of parts that are at higher risk? Can they be located? Can they be inspected for defects? Can the customers be warned not to use them in a certain way?

Developing a containment plan is one part of an eight-step process that was developed in the mid-1980s by the Ford Motor Co. for solving problems associated with field events: "TOPS 8D"—**T**eam **O**riented **P**roblem **S**olving. The TOPS 8D process is well documented and is focused on several things. It is designed to avoid drawing early and incorrect conclusions about the root cause, bring discipline to the process, and assure that long term systemic changes are made to prevent further events. The eight steps in the process are:

1. Use a team.
2. Describe the problem.
3. Develop interim containment plan.
4. Determine and verify root cause.
5. Verify permanent corrections.

6. Define and implement corrective action.
7. Prevent recurrence/system problems.
8. Congratulate the team.

However, all six decision factors—culture, goals, measurements, organizational complexity, and the perception of risk—still come into play. After all, coming up with either the containment plan or the long-term plan is still a decision process influenced by all of them.

It is particularly important to recognize that the factors of organizational complexity and perception of risk have a very strong influence on how both the containment and long-term mitigation plans get made.

Take, for example, the case of jet engines. Engines are only one part of a very complex and regulated system. Numerous other organizations such as the airplane companies, the airlines, and the FAA are involved. They, too, have to be fully involved in any decisions or plans that are made. This is a place where having a well-defined process, which spells out the roles and responsibilities of all the players, is very important.

If you combine the difficulties of perceiving risk with the confounding factor of organizational complexity, you quickly recognize how difficult it is to come up with plans that meet the requirements of all involved. Each organization has its own perception of the level of risk that is acceptable and how it should be determined.

In the aviation business, the generally accepted criteria for safety of flight is that the probability of failure should be below one chance in a billion per flight. However, determining how that criteria is met is the problem. Once again, as discussed in the last chapter, my opinion is that using probabilistic analysis based on available data should be only one of the tools used to determine an acceptable level of risk. Certainly, the potential consequences of an event must be considered as well when determining an action plan. It is also extremely important for the logo to involve the best intellectual and diverse resources at its disposal to make these judgments. Simply relying on "the numbers" is not enough.   Remember in the UA 232 case, McDonnell's assessment that the chances of all three hydraulic lines failing was less than one in a billion? Once the root cause is determined and the long-term plan is in place, the next steps in the TOPS 8D process refers to the principle, "trust but verify." Verify the corrective action works, implement the plan, and assure that the system that created the defect is fixed. We will talk a bit more about trust but verify in the next chapter.

Issues involving product safety are distinctly different than those involving unethical behavior. The TOPS 8D process described above can and should be used to formulate the long-term action plan and assure the systemic changes needed to eliminate the problem are made. However, my view is that, in cases involving ethics, the containment plan is much simpler. It must include two basic steps: (1) complete and swift disclosure to both the appropriate authorities and to those who have been affected and (2) commit to make those who have been harmed whole. Any other plan will exponentially inflate the consequences.

Look at the VW event. Initially, VW indicated the problem was due to "technical issues and unexpected test conditions," only later disclosing that there was a defeat device. Such denials will never be tolerated by the outside world and end up bringing significant legal consequences for all involved and a severe loss of reputation for the logo.

As you can see, the decision factors we have been talking about influence all the decisions that must be made to identify and address potential issues. Because of that, it is even more important to adhere to principle No. 3— make important decisions based on diverse input. Diverse perspectives, points of view, and technical knowledge counter the negative influences of the decision factors. It's imperative to tap into every available resource as there's just too much at stake to do anything less.

Chapter 19
Trust But Verify

The only thing worse than having no plan is having a solid plan that isn't carried out. At least if you have no plan, there may be reason to believe you did not know about the threat. But if you have a plan and do nothing about it, it is obvious that you knew about the threat and failed to take appropriate action. This is the reason you must not only trust, but verify as well.

Action plans are generally developed in an environment where there are numerous unknowns: Will there be hardware available? Will the customers do what we have asked them to do? How quickly will all the equipment be modified? Will the regulatory agencies accept the plan?

These are just some of the realities that arise when you are trying to implement a complex plan that involves hardware, people, and multiple organizations. Just look at the problems the car companies are facing in trying to manage the Takata airbag problem. There are millions of airbags, multiple models, regulatory agencies, governments, and the general public involved.

Once a plan is defined and agreed to, you cannot afford to assume that it will be carried out as it had been envisioned. There must be a follow-up effort that tracks implementation, and you must be ready to adjust the plan to compensate for issues that arise which threaten its success. Those people involved with assembling the mitigation plan need to stay involved to assure that the intent of the original plan is preserved. I still reflect on the advice the chief engineer gave me to inspect fan discs prior to UA 232, and thinking that we may have missed a chance to prevent the accident had he followed up on his recommendation.

One of the elements of the product safety policy we put in place at GE Aircraft Engines required the creation of a worklist for each program. That worklist provided a means to tracking the safety concerns that were raised and the progress of the plans that were put in place to mitigate the threats. The work lists are reviewed on a regular basis so that adjustments can be made to the plan as new situations arise.

It is important to recognize that this type of verification process is required at all levels. Reviewing program status relative to the plan should be done regularly, at least quarterly, at the working level and reviewed a minimum of annually at the logo level. Combine the reviews with notification to the logo level every time a significant change to the implementation plan occurs. Remember, a plan not executed will be judged harshly by the outside world. Monday morning quarterbacks salivate at the thought of saying, "You knew about the risk and didn't follow up."

Another part of this trust-but-verify philosophy is monitoring the decision process itself. At GE Aircraft Engines, we were sure to have a member of the Flight Safety Organization be a member of the working level teams. Their role was not only to bring their expertise and perspectives to the decision process, but to serve as a process monitor. As chief engineer, I was always sure to keep track of how the process was working and made it a point to attend as many working level meetings as I could. I used these meetings not only as an opportunity to add my perspective to the process, but to get a sense at how well that process was working. If there was a problem, I knew I could count on the very topmost management of the organization to address them. This is the benefit of being part of an open organization that has the right culture and values. Without these, having a doomsday event is only a matter of time.

Chapter 20
The Personal Side of the Personal World

In Chapter 15, I described the three worlds—the outside world, the corporate world, and the personal world—and explained how doomsday events not only had consequences for the corporate world but for the personal world as well. I have experienced this myself, as the UA 232 event led to some very significant personal consequences.

If a person chooses to act unethically, there is an expectation that if and when they are caught that there will be consequences. They might not be happy they were caught, but more often than not there will not be a significant psychological impact. However, if you consider yourself well-intentioned, responsible, and concerned about the welfare of others, being involved in an event which causes bodily harm has other, longer-lasting effects. This is what happened to me. In retrospect, I believe it is the reason why I wanted to write this book.

I certainly am not a graduate of the Harvard Business School, nor am I an expert on the psychology of how people make decisions. But I believe my own involvement in the UA 232 event has given me a particularly unique perspective. I hope my experience might be motivation for others who might find themselves in a position to make decisions which could potentially save others' lives.

Seared forever into my memory is the moment when the metallurgist that I had been working with on the hard alpha problem showed me the cut-up of the fan disc that was manufactured from the same billet as the failed disc. I can still picture him walking across the parking lot with it in his hand. When I saw the microstructure, we both looked at each other and knew the problem that we had been working on for several years was the cause of the accident. That's when reality set in: the problem I had been working on as an engineering problem suddenly became a problem that cost 111 people their lives. There are no words to describe the impact that something like that has on you. Before the accident, work was work, and outside of work was outside of work. Suddenly, my personal world and my corporate world were forever intertwined.

It got worse once the litigation began. In Chicago, after being deposed for about two days, one of the plaintiff's lawyers asked the question: "In light of the fact that the engine would explode, that there is no way to contain the fan disk in the event of a failure, can we agree that any risk of failure on a titanium rotating part is unreasonable and unacceptable …" This is when I understood how the outside world fits into the picture. I can attest, that to this day, the wound from that question has never healed. What I learned from that is that the outside world judges not only the corporate world but the personal world as well. Even if people in the outside world don't know all the circumstances involved in making the decisions leading up to the event, they will make judgments based on whether those decisions made sense, were not self-serving, and took the wellbeing of the user into account as the highest priority. Anything less than that will lead to the harshest of all possible consequences for everyone involved. I can also say with conviction that years after the event, you will continue to judge yourself by the same standards.

As I have reflected back on UA 232, every once in a while I would go to the internet and Google what I might find about the accident. I came upon a YouTube video of a documentary made by Errol Morris called, "Leaving This Earth—Denny Fitch–DC-10 Pilot and Hero." It was a four-part video featuring Captain Denny Fitch, who was the United Airlines training check airman on flight UA 232.

Captain Fitch was dead-heading home from Salt Lake City when the disc failed. Captain Haines called him up to the cockpit to manipulate the throttles on the two remaining engines. Since all the hydraulic lines were severed, that turned out to be the only way the airplane could be controlled.

I encourage you to watch the video as it brings a personal perspective to the event that can't be captured any other way. At about 11:08 minutes in to Part IV of the video, Captain Fitch describes the scene in the hospital after the accident: His wife comes in to see him and he asks her how many of the passengers survived. She tells him that 111 people did not make it.

His reaction was remarkable. He actually felt guilty for not doing better! This, coming from a man who just did what was judged to be impossible because, after the accident, other crews tried 28 times in the simulator to land the plane and failed.

I, too, look back on the UA 232 event and ask myself if I could have done better. The answer is yes. Yes, there were others involved. Yes, there were other chances to break the chain of events. But when I look back at what I did and what I knew, I can't help but feel guilty for missing my chance to do it. That's the personal side of the personal world.

Chapter 21
If You Read Nothing Else, Read This

As I said at the beginning of this book, I have always been infatuated with anything aviation. It has always been a passion and has provided me with an exceptional opportunity to work in an environment that I loved. But, in retrospect, what I didn't expect is what the aviation world would teach me about the process of making decisions. What I learned is in the aviation environment, decisions really, really matter! They matter for several reasons.

The first is risk. You cannot expect to fly at 35,000 feet in an aluminum tube, in all kinds of weather, over the oceans, without any risk! It is impossible. You learn this very quickly flying your own single engine plane into bad weather that you decided was "not so bad" before you took to the sky. That decision that you made on the ground before the flight immediately threatens your life and the life of anyone else on the airplane. I made a few of those decisions and quickly came to regret them. Those experiences bring home the reality that the aviation environment is unforgiving of a poor decision-making process.

The second is responsibility. I can't describe to you how you feel when you get yourself into one of those situations that I described above and look over at your wife sitting in the right seat. You have made a decision that not only threatened your own life but hers as well. If you watch the Captain Fitch video you will see how seriously he took responsibility for the lives of his passengers.

When I began my career at GE, I didn't think about those kinds of things. I was too interested in the technology, the designs, the numbers, and doing the best technical job that I could. I simply did not feel the weight of the responsibility that comes with the aviation environment.

Then came UA 232! Everything changed. Suddenly, I realized that people's lives directly depended on what I did as an engineer and what my company did as an organization. That is when the personal world and the corporate world came together.

But there were many people who worked on that problem. Why should I feel like I was responsible? The disc was made years before; It was melted by a contractor; United Airlines inspected it before the failure; and so on and so on. Nobody has ever blamed me personally. But, I knew I did not carry out the chief engineer's recommendation to ultrasonically inspect fan discs. And because of that, we may have missed an opportunity to prevent the accident and save 111 lives.

I can tell you that it doesn't make any difference what the circumstances were or who else might have been involved. If you are involved with an event that takes the lives of others you will carry that burden with you for the rest of your life.

I have turned 75 this year and when you get to this point you look back and ask yourself: What did I accomplish? What did I regret? And what did I leave behind?

I am proud of many of the technical things I did during my years at GE. I worked with the best and brightest people on the most advanced technology. I had a chance to see many of the things I worked on power airplanes like the B-1 Bomber, the F-14, and F-16 fighters, and many of

168

the airplanes in commercial service today. The work was exciting, challenging, and fun. It doesn't get better than that.

Certainly, throughout a 38-year career you regret a number of things, but for me, there is only one thing that stands out and that I will never forget—my decision not to pursue the fan disc inspection program.

So, what I leave behind is this book. Unfortunately, there is no easy way to make that magic decision that will prevent all events. The world is just too complicated and uncertain. However, I am a strong believer that if organizations and the people in them adhere to the principles in Chapter 9, the likelihood of experiencing such events will be greatly reduced.

With that, I would like to finish with a summary of those principles and a bit of advice:

Clearly communicate the values of the enterprise

The role of upper management is to communicate the values of the enterprise. This must be done often and by actions as well as words. It is up to them to make it the foundation of the organization's culture. They also must make it clear when they are communicating goals that they are not to be met at the expense of those values—the balanced decision.

Build and nurture the "right" culture

The "right" culture is open and communicative—both up and down. It also must be one where everyone's input is respected and seriously considered by management. Without this, employees will be reluctant to raise potential issues.

Always get diverse input when making critical decisions

My biggest regret when I look back to the UA 232 event is that I made the "not to inspect" decision alone. The fundamental purpose behind this principle is to avoid decisions that, in hindsight, look dumb. Getting the input of others leverages the intellects and perspectives of those participating in the decision-making process, and is a powerful tool to address the important perception of risk factor.

Trust, but verify

Nothing happens the way it is planned. Follow-up and tracking need to be an integral part of any organization's decision-making process.

The logo is responsible so the logo should make the decision

Whatever the process, any critical decision should have been made by those who are responsible for meeting the responsibilities, values, and goals of the organization. This is only possible if the right culture exists.

Define individual and organizational roles and responsibilities

Everyone needs to know how the decision process works and how they can participate. They also need to know that it will be carried out fairly and without retribution for those who have a different point of view.

And the advice:

For management: Everyone in the organization is listening and watching what you say and do. When you set goals, people in the organization may react to them in ways you do not want or expect. Be sure to always reinforce that goals are never to be achieved at the expense of values.

For employees: The chain of events which lead up to doomsday events is made up of a series of small links. You may be the one who either creates a link or has the opportunity to break one. You create a link by not doing the best that you can. You miss an opportunity if you don't raise issues. Just because you are just a small cog in a big wheel does not mean that you will not suffer consequences should a doomsday event occur.

For all: There is no easy way to make hard decisions. Never try to do it alone. Seek the advice and counsel of those you respect and who understand both the circumstances and the risks for the organization. If I leave you with just one message, it is that diversity of thought is the best way to make decisions which avoid the doomsday event.

About the Author

Fred Herzner is the retired chief engineer of General Electric Aircraft Engines, a position he held from 1995 to 2003. In that role, he had responsibility for assuring that the engineering design processes reflected the best practices of the business, managing the flight safety organization, and being the liaison between the aircraft engine business and various industry groups and regulatory agencies.

Herzner contributed to numerous engine programs, both military and commercial, ranging from advanced technology demonstrators to many of the engines that are in service today. These included engines for aircraft like the B1-B Bomber, the F-16 and F-15 Fighters, the MD-11, B-737, B-767, B-747, A-320, A-300, A-310, and A-330, among others. He is the holder of several patents. In addition, his contributions to the aircraft engines business were recognized with the Perry T. Egbert award for engineering excellence and his induction into GE Aviation's Hall of Fame.

In his role as chief engineer and manager of the flight safety organization, Herzner was instrumental in formulating and implementing a formal company policy on how to identify and address issues which could potentially have flight safety implications. That policy reflected Herzner's experience gained from his involvement in programs designed to address in service issues and his "pilot's perspective" learned from flying his own aircraft.

After his retirement, he continued to do engineering consulting work, both at GE and other companies involved in the aircraft engines business.

Herzner holds both a bachelor's degree in aerospace

engineering and a master's degree in applied mechanics from The Polytechnic Institute of Brooklyn. Herzner is a licensed pilot with instrument and commercial ratings. He has been involved in all phases of aviation from building model airplanes as a boy to owning, building, and flying his own airplanes all over the country.